THE SINKING OF THE
LUSITANIA

UNRA   TERIES

PATRICK O'SULLIVAN

The Collins Press

PUBLISHED IN 2014 BY
The Collins Press
West Link Park
Doughcloyne
Wilton
Cork

A CIP record for this book is available from the British Library.

Paperback ISBN: 978-1-84889-2156
PDF eBook ISBN: 978-1-84889-8684
EPUB eBook ISBN: 978-1-84889-8707
Kindle ISBN: 978-1-84889-8691

Typesetting by Carrigboy Typesetting Services
Typeset in Garamond
Printed in Malta by Gutenberg Press Limited

Contents

Contents

Acknowledgments

TO ATTEMPT TO WRITE A BOOK about an event that occurred almost a hundred years ago at first seems a daunting task. However, the encouragement and help I received from institutions and persons, and their willingness to respond to requests, has made such a book possible. I am very grateful to all of these people; some contributed a vast amount of information, while others offered a single piece of specialised information or suggested a rainbow that often led to a crock of gold.

I owe an immeasurable debt of gratitude to my late colleague and friend John Light of Boston. Without John's contribution, chapters eight and nine of this book could not have been written. I am indebted to Muriel Light and her family for permission to quote from John's findings relating to aluminium powder and munitions. Sadly, Muriel passed away in December 1997, before this book's completion. The multitudinous documentation sent to me by John Light has relieved me of a great burden in searching the records to unearth data. I am especially indebted to Mrs Beesly for granting me permission to quote from the private letters of the late Patrick Beesly (to John Light) with regard to British Intelligence in 1915 and the machinations of Room 40. Patrick Beesly's book of the same name is pre-requisite reading for any serious student of the *Lusitania* story. I would like to thank Mr Hibberd of the Imperial War Museum for providing solutions to major problems in relation to shrapnel on the *Lusitania,* and detailed information on the use of aluminium fine powder for explosives manufacture at the Royal Laboratory at Woolwich in support of the 1914–18 war. Mr Hibberd deciphered numbers, notations and weights indicated on the *Lusitania*'s munitions invoices, and explained, in plain language, their true meaning. I am also indebted to Larry Dorgan, former CQMS 11th Infantry Division Irish Army, and his then colleague CS Gus O'Donnell. These gentlemen contributed greatly to my knowledge of First World War artillery shells, shrapnel and percussion fuses.

I wish to thank Oceaneering Contractors and their team for inviting me on board their diving vessel *Archimedes* during their 1982 diving exploration of the *Lusitania*. I want to thank Oceaneering diver Frank Mulcahy, who loaned me brass percussion fuses, which he recovered from the wreck and in which he allowed me to drill holes for inspection purposes, to validate their inert nature. I wish to thank *National*

Acknowledgments

Geographic and Bruce Norfleet for inviting me as a guest to witness their exciting film work on the *Lusitania* in 1993. Also Bob Ballard for allowing me to tour the *Lusitania* in the armchair comfort of his control module on board the ROV support ship, *Northern Horizon*. I wish to thank *National Geographic* consultants Eric and Bill Sauder whose knowledge of vintage liners and photographic archive of *Lusitania* pictures are second to none. I am enriched by having met these two specialists during their visit to Ireland, and privileged to have shared their knowledge and valued opinions. I would like to thank the London Technical Diving Team, led by Polly Tapson, for their valued diving observations in the vicinity of forward cargo hatches numbers one and two on the *Lusitania*'s foredeck, and survey carried out on portions of number one boiler room. I would like to acknowledge Tim Cadogan, former Cork County Librarian, for making available much-valued material for my Queenstown chapter and also for details relevant to rescue craft. I would like to thank Mr Dermot Lucey MA, of Cork, for allowing me to quote from his paper *Lusitania Shock Waves*. This valuable paper provides insight into the mood and attitude of the people in Ireland around the time of the disaster. I would like to thank fellow *Lusitania* author, and military historian, Graham Maddocks of Liverpool for his valued comments and contribution to my book. Chris Doncaster of Sheffield provided the entire story of the Manx fishing boat *Wanderer* and the heroic role it played in the rescue of survivors. I would like to thank Noel Ray, Luke Cassidy and Geoff Whitfield of the Cobh Titanic Society for providing information and statistics on the Queenstown dead following the loss of the *Lusitania*. Michael Galvin kindly allowed me to quote from his book *Black Blight*. My gratitude to Mr John James of Kinsale for bringing to my attention his sensational discovery of yet another variation of a *Lusitania* medal lampooning British propaganda in Sweden. Doctor John De Courcy Ireland kindly gave me a copy of Lieutenant Weisbach's hand-written account of his experiences inside the U-20 as it stalked and torpedoed the *Lusitania*; he also read my final manuscript and suggested some additions which I have since included in this book. I am indebted to Doctor Paul Cartwright of the Chillworth Technology and Research Centre of Southampton; this company was most generous in making available scientific data on the explosibility of aluminium fine powder. I would like to thank chemical engineers Ron Klaus, of Eli Lilly, for providing me with instructions that enabled me to fabricate a dust-cloud explosion test chamber and Barry Welch, also of Eli Lilly, for much scientific data on aluminium. Michael O'Connell of Micro Mist also made a substantial contribution to my bulging aluminium file. I wish to acknowledge the Bureau of Mines in Pittsburgh for providing a detailed paper on the ability of aluminium powder to produce hydrogen gas when brought into contact with water. Finally, I wish to thank Paddy Duggan, chemistry teacher, for hazarding the science laboratory of Bandon Vocational School, and possibly his job, by running test experiments on aluminium powder's potential to explode violently.

I would like to acknowledge the following institutions: the Bundesarchiv, Koblenz; the Merseyside Maritime Museum; the National Maritime Museum; St Petersburg Maritime Museum; the Scottish Records Office; the National Archives, Washington; Liverpool University; the Franklin D. Roosevelt Library, New York; Cork County Library; the Public Records Office, Kew; the Royal Navy Submarine Museum, Gosport; Trinity College, Dublin; the Imperial War Museum, London; Glasgow University; and the British Museum.

I am indebted to Commander Richard Compton-Hall RN, author of several books on submarines, and Britain's foremost authority on 1915 submarines. Richard provided me with a fascinating insight into the appalling conditions of squalor and discomfort endured daily by submariners of the Great War. Richard was an ex-submariner and wrote a definitive book on J.P. Holland, the Irish submarine inventor. I would like to acknowledge Alan Roddie for much expertise and computer wizardry in scanning and adjusting my text to meet 21st-century publisher requirements and for research in TCD archives on my behalf. I would like to thank renowned author Eddie Burke for researching the Robson papers at Trinity College, Dublin, on my behalf. I am indebted to ex-*Lusitania* diver Ciaran Dempsey for bringing to my attention an anomaly on the sea bed aft of the *Lusitania*. This has yet to be explored and may hold vital evidence regarding the second explosion on the liner. I would like to thank Michael O'Brien of Butlerstown, a veritable walking data-bank on maritime affairs, for bringing many relevant books to my attention; also Raymond White for background information on Captain Dow of the *Lusitania,* and David Griffiths of Castle Bernard who provided much useful data on Churchill. In conclusion, I am indebted to my London proofreader, Keith Good, for his meticulous attention to detail – Keith applied his shammy on numerous occasions to bring a high lustre to otherwise dull sections of my book. Finally, I would like to thank my wife Del for selflessly putting down her book or forfeiting her favourite television programme to read over my meandering story line, and for offering much valued criticism and suggestions on how it should be presented in a more comprehensible way. Without Del's efforts, portions of my story would be meaningless and confusing; in making these corrections, Del inadvertently became Ireland's most authoritative housewife on the *Lusitania* story.

Preface

Much of great value has already been written about the *Lusitania* and its tragic demise off the Old Head of Kinsale. Regrettably, some writers have chosen to cloud the story in fiction and then pass off the fruits of their imaginations to the reader as facts. Such writers have realised the magnetic power of sensationalism to attract the reader's attention, and have shown much flair in inventing bizarre stories around the great liner; the mixture of fact and fiction written about the *Lusitania* has tended to leave the reader bewildered and confused. These issues will be addressed, and in doing so, will unravel many of the mysteries surrounding its history. In portraying the story of the *Lusitania* against its wartime background, the fog of confusion is lifted from the otherwise inexplicable actions taken by the Cunard Company and the British Admiralty.

This book attempts to stimulate further investigations of the *Lusitania* by identifying new unexplored avenues of research in relation to vital missing telegrams sent specifically from the Admiralty to the *Lusitania* during her last hours of active service on the Atlantic Ocean. Further diving visits to the desolate wilderness of scrap iron, which is now the *Lusitania* wreck, will add vital pieces to the ongoing story, and the recovery of shrapnel and other munitions will validate theories expounded herein. It is hoped that the Dublin authorities will reconsider their stance in preventing recovery of certain historical artefacts from the cargo hatches of the *Lusitania*. Such recovered objects belong on the shelves of museums where they will bring enlightenment about the past and enhance our appreciation of our maritime heritage.

This book compares the fate of the *Lusitania* to that of at least six other lesser-known liners which also ran the gauntlet of war. Staggering tales of inefficiency and blundering in the corridors of power are also brought to the reader's attention. Intelligence mistakes in relation to the *Lusitania* incident were repeated one year later in the Battle of Jutland, in which 6,000 British servicemen lost their lives in a one-day sea battle.

As author I invite you, dear reader, to share my long voyage through one of the most fascinating stories of the Great War at sea.

Introduction

Growing up no more than a handful of miles from the south coast of Ireland in the late 1950s, it was difficult to escape hearing old fishermen tales of the German U-boats that stalked our shores during the 1914–18 war. Tales of merchant ships being committed to watery graves, almost daily by submarines, were endless. In February 1915 Germany gave the world notice of her intended blockade of the British Isles which was later implemented by the U-boats in a war against merchant shipping. The submarine commanders found the waters between Fastnet and Waterford to be especially rich in targets in their devastating campaign to cut off Britain's supplies and starve her into submission.

At the age of eighteen I embarked on a career of commercial diving. The skills acquired were put to good use in my leisure time by diving to countless casualties of the Great War; the thrill of visiting this vast graveyard of rusting shipwrecks stimulated my interest in cataloguing and researching the tragic story of each one. It was inevitable that my gaze would eventually fall on our most fascinating and tragic shipwreck, the *Lusitania.* In early years little was known about the *Lusitania,* as time seemed to have dimmed the memory of her tragic loss. Books about the great liner were available, though many were flawed for lack of information, and others depended mainly on newspaper cuttings. The diving technology of the day precluded any visits to the wreck because its extreme depth of over 300 feet was far in excess of the safe limits of air diving equipment. Deep-diving technology involving mixed gas and saturation chamber procedures was still at the experimental stage by the American Navy and others, and not available to the wider commercial diving market. Yet another difficulty was the fact that nobody seemed to know the exact position of the wreck, though it had been located by Captain Russell of the *Orphir* in 1935. However, the *Lusitania* was soon to be roused from its long sleep with the arrival in Kinsale of the swashbuckling ex-US Navy diver, John Light and his team. In 1959 John Light achieved record-breaking status by diving using aqualung and compressed air to a depth of 300 feet while filming a submarine escape exercise for the US Navy. Having ended a navy career he joined NBC Television News as a freelance underwater cameraman. NBC were keen to film the remains of the *Lusitania* and their new-found freelance diving photographer seemed to be the ideal man for the job. John wished to see at first hand if the accusations of guns and munitions on board the *Lusitania* were true. If such evidence could be located, he would film it as proof of the liner's dual role of passenger ship and gunrunner. Captain Henry Russell, who had first located the *Lusitania,* gladly gave the co-ordinates to the American divers and urged them to obtain a Decca navigator to assist them in their search for the wreck. The newly-arrived American divers set up base camp in Kinsale, which was then a sleepy old fishing town steeped in antiquity.

John Light and his team commenced diving to the *Lusitania* in 1960 and concluded operations in 1962. In total the team logged forty-two dives to the wreck using standard compressed air at a depth regarded as being far beyond the limits of human safety. The intense pressure at such depths caused the divers to suffer mind-numbing narcosis. Perishing water was another problem to contend with due to the shortcomings of neoprene diving suits; poor lighting conditions on the wreck required very powerful floodlighting to make photography possible. As the lamps were supplied with power from the surface, the divers had the added problem of wrestling with heavy and cumbersome cables that were prone to being snagged on the wreck.

The black-and-white film shot on the wreck was of extremely poor quality and reflected the limits of underwater photography at that time. High wind and intermittent Atlantic gales also robbed the divers of valuable working days. The financial burden of these early efforts was shouldered by NBC who were in alliance with BBC on the venture. During his stay in Kinsale, John Light was struck by Cupid's arrow when he met, and subsequently married, the beautiful Muriel Acton of the renowned Actons Hotel family. In spite of his superhuman efforts on the *Lusitania,* no guns or munitions were located and his findings were unsensational to say the least. Diving operations finally petered out toward the end of 1962 and the Light family departed from these shores as the *Lusitania* once again faded into obscurity. In the years that followed, big changes were occurring in the diving world. Toward the late 1960s, the need to discover new sources of gas and oil prompted exploration companies to look towards the North Sea for alternative supplies. Such exploration could only be carried out with support of deep diving-systems which were still in the embryonic stages of their development. In the clamour by oil companies to explore the ocean's oil reserves, vast sums of money became available to hasten such development. Existing mixed gas diving techniques were improved and perfected. Divers could now work at great depths using helium gas to rid them of stupefying nitrogen narcosis: hot water diving suits eliminated problems of cold water, and saturation chambers allowed divers unlimited time working on the sea bed. At last, diving had been dragged into the twentieth century. These sudden and dramatic changes did not go unnoticed by John Light, who wished to apply them to his beloved *Lusitania*.

In 1967, he successfully sought financial backing from the American publishing house of Holt, Rinehart & Winston and purchased the wreck of the *Lusitania* for £1,000 from the War Risk Association of Liverpool. As War Risk had no equity in the cargo, John Light was reminded that he had no claim to them and could only assume ownership of the hull and machinery. Most of the cargo was Ministry of Defence property and private goods, including a hoard of mythical oil paintings, were insured on the open market. A proviso was also inserted that on completion of the sale, the new owner would be responsible for any future liabilities or expenses that might be attached to the wreck. On completion of the transaction, John Light and his family once again returned to Kinsale to initiate a new programme of diving and discovery. He first purchased a 90-foot wooden Scottish trawler named the *Doonie Braes* which he personally captained from Edinburgh to Kinsale.

Conversion of the Scottish trawler to diving vessel commenced off Kinsale pier; however, the pledged financial support of the publishing house was almost expended and more money was needed to continue. A new backer, Boston building contractor George Macomber, stepped in and promised to finance the venture. The Scottish trawler was now relegated to redundancy and a much larger French steel trawler named *Kinvarra* was purchased as plans became more ambitious. It was hoped to build and install a saturation diving complex on board the *Kinvarra,* now tied up to the pier. The Swiss scientist, Hans Keller, was engaged as a consultant to supervise operations. At first a trickle of crates and packages began to arrive at Kinsale pier. The trickle soon became a torrent as various diving chambers, helium cylinder banks, high pressure gas equipment, compressors, television monitors, carbon dioxide scrubbers, underwater lighting, gas reclaim systems, hydraulic equipment, cameras, gas analysers and highly sophisticated diving apparatus arrived. Gangs of shipbuilders, engineers and technicians swarmed aboard daily to assemble this complex technological jigsaw and convert the *Kinvarra* to a state-of-the-art salvage vessel and dive-support ship. The blue flash of the welder's torch, the constant chipping of hammers, the whirring of drilling machines, the whining of angle grinders and the jostling of dock cranes all bore testimony to the bedlam below decks as the workers laboured in their cramped compartments. Oxy-acetylene cutting gear would sporadically burst into flames and shower the deck with golden sparks as an unwanted beam was cut away, or a bulkhead pierced to allow the passage of pipes or electric cables. The media attended in droves in anticipation of recording some great *Lusitania* discovery that might happen at any moment.

In essence John Light was attempting to build a prototype diving complex in the bowels of the *Kinvarra*. Many parts sought were not off-the-shelf items and had to be specially built. Major components from gas chromatographs to high-pressure valving failed to work as claimed, and were either returned to their suppliers or modified on board. Planned diving schedules were routinely postponed, and deadlines were pushed into the future as interminable delays and problems occurred daily. The result was that the *Kinvarra* barely left the pier over a one-year period and not a single dive was made to explore the *Lusitania* with the new technology that promised so much. Mr Macomber became apprehensive as cost overruns became rampant and another investor by the name of Gregg Bemis was introduced to share the financial burden. By December 1969, an estimated $500,000 had been spent and the jaded backers still saw no prospect of any immediate return for their money. A decision was taken to liquidate the operation. John Light was suddenly out of a job and his plans lay in shambles; the now much-publicised *Kinvarra* was towed to Amsterdam in November 1969 and its associated company, Kinvarra Shipping, voted into liquidation in 1970. The *Kinvarra* was subsequently gutted and sold off; thus ended the fiasco.

John Light and his family lingered in Kinsale until 1973, and John's attention was again focused on research with a view to writing a book. Eventually the whole family departed for London where John researched extensively for two years from March 1973 with sponsorship by NBC, who had backed his work on and off over a fifteen-year period. A future film was discussed in conjunction with fresh discoveries which John hoped to make in British archives. In this capacity, his true talent as a brilliant researcher and investigator came to the fore. Light threw himself into the drudgery of archival work and was unrelenting in his pursuit of relevant documents that might unlock some of the mysteries surrounding the *Lusitania*.

Unwittingly, he chartered a parallel course to that of two other *Lusitania* greats; namely Captain Roskill, Britain's official naval historian for the Second World War and Patrick Beesly, author of several books including a monumental study of British Intelligence in the 1914–18 war. The trio met from time to time to debate their intriguing findings. Churchill became the central character of Light's study, with Captain Reginald Hall running closely behind. If the British Admiralty had engaged in dirty tricks in regard to the loss of the *Lusitania,* then the first Lord of the Admiralty, Winston Churchill, must have initiated such activity. At every opportunity, John Light made a point of visiting the descendants of his *Lusitania* characters, including the families of Reginald Hall, Lord Mersey and various descendants of officers from the *Lusitania*. He also paid visits to Miss Mabel Every, Captain Turner's housekeeper and companion.

This policy bore fruit as he was often given access to private family papers not in the public domain. His odyssey through the archives was often frustrated by emasculated files, empty folders, and tantalising references or information that could not be made available to him as it was still classified in the national interest. John believed that much evidence had been destroyed in the past as part of a cover-up.

While John Light had achieved little in his chilly forays to the bottom of the Atlantic off Kinsale, he now made real discoveries in the dusty shelves of the archives. Light had a sixth sense about where he might find some answers to the many riddles, and persistently coaxed and persuaded the British authorities to release classified information regarding U-boat wireless intercepts and naval staff monographs. In this quest he had limited success but yet enough to discover sensational new information. John's exhaustive study in Britain only mirrored his trojan researches at the American end. In the United States, he researched extensively in the National Archives, Washington DC, the Office of US Naval Intelligence, the National Archives and Records Administration, New York, the Library of Congress and Yale University Library to mention but a few. In all, he accumulated 15,000 documents as material to help him write a definitive book. In the scholarly book, *Lusitania Disaster* by Ryan and Bailey, Light is given abundant accreditation for his help and for providing the authors with an immense amount of material. In Patrick Beesly's book, *Room 40,* Light is again acknowledged and heaped with praise for the extensive part he played in making its *Lusitania* chapter possible.

Captain Roskill was stunned by John Light's findings, especially as he produced information that Captain Roskill had long assumed to have been destroyed. Colin Simpson's book about the *Lusitania* began as a Light-Simpson collaboration in 1973 when John Light was in financial doldrums. A dispute followed and resulted in Simpson writing his own book. John was very scathing of Simpson's book and later wrote a critique of its inaccuracies. Sadly John Light passed away on 19 May 1992 and his intended book never materialised. His extensive archive is in the private possession of his family and one hopes it will some day be turned over to an appreciative university or library.

I, the author, joined John Light as a twenty-two year-old diver in 1967, the era of the *Kinvarra* debacle. A strong friendship was struck between myself and his family, and it was perhaps inevitable that I, too, would succumb to the *Lusitania* virus. Over the next twenty-five years, I barraged John with an endless stream of letters, telephone calls and queries about the disaster. He was always abundantly generous in providing answers that were backed up by sources as well as photocopies of material from his personal collection. I was privileged to have shared his innermost thoughts and theories and now feel that fate has bestowed on me a caretaker role in which to write a book about the *Lusitania* in John Light's memory. Some of his sensational discoveries are revealed in this book, in particular the most compelling theory to date on the cause of the second mysterious explosion to which he attributed the rapid loss of the great liner.

The Hymn of the *Lusitania*

The swift sea sucks her death-shriek under
As the great ship reels and leaps asunder.
Crammed taffrail-high with her murderous freight,
Like a straw on the tide she whirls to her fate.
A warship she, though she lacked its coat,
And lustful for lives as none afloat,
A warship, and one of the foe's best workers,
Not penned with her rusty harbour-shirkers.
Now the Flanders guns lack their deadly bread,
And shipper and buyer are sick with dread,
For neutral as Uncle Sam may be
Your surest neutral is the deep green sea.
Just one ship sunk, with lives and shell
And thousands of German gray-coats well!
And for each of her gray-coats, German hate
Would have sunk ten ships with all their freight,
Yea, ten such ships are a paltry fine
For one good life in our fighting line.
Let England ponder the crimson text:
Torpedo, strike! and hurrah the next.

This German poem was translated by a Mrs Wharton
and a copy given to Theodore Roosevelt.

1

Gathering War Clouds

IN EXPLORING THE STORY of the *Lusitania*, it is important to understand how the political and economic climate affected the events leading to the sinking of this passenger liner. The early years of the century were dominated by the Great War of 1914–18. This mighty clash of empires involved such countries as Britain, Germany, America, Belgium, France, Turkey, Iraq, Japan, Bulgaria, Italy, Austria, China and Russia amongst others. Tens of thousands of innocent neutrals were also caught in the cross-fire and suffered great hardship and loss of life. Unlike earlier wars, in which the horse played a vital role in moving men and machinery, the steamship and railroad had now been perfected and could move large armies and equipment to the four corners of the earth.

The Great War was the first to use the new means of communication: wireless telegraphy as developed by Marconi. Once at sea, naval units could now communicate with their bases or with other units at sea. The march of science and technology saw new weapons of destruction that could inflict slaughter and devastation on an unheard-of scale; the war became a consuming flame around the world, causing losses to victors and vanquished out of all proportion to the issues involved. New technology changed the methods of warfare profoundly; long-range guns had been developed which could sink ships at twelve miles distant. The newly-invented aeroplane made its debut in the Great War and evolved rapidly over the four-year period. The submarine, torpedo and mine were all new weapons. The German Zeppelins entered the arena to provide valuable reconnaissance and could bomb targets from the air. Poison gas was used to add to the horrors of the land war in the trenches of Europe; the tank also made its debut as a means of countering the stalemate in the trenches.

Land armies were millions strong, supported by entire populations who organised food supplies and munitions for the Front; able-bodied men throughout Europe were called to their armies or navies in great numbers and were replaced in the factories by women. Concern for civilian safety during shelling and bombing soon dissipated as the war plumbed new depths of horror daily until it became a free-for-all. The air offensive was the most revolutionary of all the new methods and increased in range and terror with every new month of the war; great areas of Europe were now subject to nightly attack by bombs being dropped from aeroplanes and Zeppelins. Cities such as London and Paris passed sleepless nights as the bombs burst around them; these attacks were countered by anti-aircraft guns which made an intolerable racket as they tried to shoot down the aeroplanes. Fire engines and ambulances raced through the streets to deal with fires and treat the injured and dying. The effects of this were especially distressing to the civilian population.

The land war was soon bogged down in the mud and barbed wire of the trenches in Europe as opposing armies were locked in stalemate; slaughter on both sides was inflicted daily on a relentless scale. In a single day, during the Battle of the Somme, over 20,000 soldiers lost their lives to shell and bullet. The war at sea saw the ruthless campaign of unrestricted submarine warfare bring Britain to her knees. As U-boat terror peaked in April 1917, Allied shipping was being committed to the bottom of the ocean at a rate of half a million tons per month; Britain had only six weeks of food left and was within a hair's breadth of surrender. Throughout the four years of horror, food production had dwindled to a trickle. Various governments took possession of what remained and imposed severe rationing on the population. The year 1918 saw general world-wide shortages of food and other essentials such as clothing and housing. Factories, business and economic life were disrupted; roads and railways were ruptured or ceased to exist. As a result of the war, new frontiers and boundaries were created, cutting off traditional routes between countries.

The war ended in November of 1918 with the general mutiny of the German Navy at their base in Kiel as well as food riots in towns and cities in Germany. All parties were reduced to exhaustion and demoralisation; towards the end of 1918, the populace were dealt another major blow in the form of pestilence. Europe was enduring a partial state of famine and general ill-health when an influenza virus struck and wiped out an estimated twelve million lives world-wide compared to eight million lives lost in action during the war. The end of the war saw the loss of four great empires, namely the Russian, Ottoman, Austro-Hungarian and German empires as centuries-old monarchies were extinguished. Before leaving the subject, it is necessary to look in more detail at the reasons for the war and events in so far as they concerned Germany, since it was Germany's actions which precipitated the building of a series of great British four-funnel liners, including the *Lusitania*.

There were a myriad of reasons for the First World War, many stemming from centuries-old antagonisms, rooted in religious, economic, social, territorial and trade conflicts. While the war burst forth in 1914, it was expected as far back as the 1870s. Germany had suffered an extended period of economic difficulties from 1870 to 1890, and noted that countries like

Britain and France were adept at spinning the globe and usurping large unnamed countries, mainly in Africa and Asia, and usually taking the lion's share.

The twentieth century was to be the era of colonial empire-building, and Germany wished to be in on the act. The German Kaiser wished to have his 'place in the sun' and expand his meagre overseas possessions. Even as early as 1890, Germany felt she had already missed the boat in the game of empire building. One politician in the German Reich warned that if it did not act soon the only land available would be on the moon. Many felt that the failure of Germany to acquire a sizeable bloc of colonies spelt disaster for her future; without an empire of its own, Germany's industry would always be dependent on other great powers. These other nations might introduce protectionist policies, and exclude Germany from their markets, or discriminate against it in other political ways, as free trade was already in decline in the world market-place. As Germany's markets were controlled politically by others, great concern was felt by its industrialists. Germany felt a great need to adopt a global policy that would take it into the world market. It saw little alternative to the notion of expand or suffocate. History had shown that the status of a great colonial power required a great navy to back it up; Germany did not have such a navy in spite of having one of the greatest land armies in Europe. Without a navy, Germany could not assert itself in international politics and could not rise to world power status. The German Secretary of State, Alfred Von Tirpitz, calculated that Britain, with the finest navy in the world, was a stumbling block that threatened German aspirations. Without a navy, Germany could not acquire new territories without the tacit approval of the British. Von Tirpitz also stated in 1909 that Germany could not expect fair play from Britain until its navy was in place. The Royal Navy could force Germany to abandon her political demands or face defeat in war. Without a navy, Germany could not take countermeasures and her industrial power and wealth appeared to be built on sand as long as Britannia ruled the waves. Germany was vexed also by potentially dangerous internal and external problems; the building of a new navy, as well as a global policy, was seen as a panacea for all Germany's domestic and foreign problems and would also secure the survival of the monarchy. Such a navy could be used as a political lever against other nations to help extract territorial concessions as well as providing a safeguard for existing possessions. It was also believed that it would revive patriotism of the classes and fill them with loyalty to their emperor and country.

With the active backing of Kaiser Wilhelm II, Von Tirpitz's campaign to secure support from the public for his new navy finally bore fruit. Huge sums of money were provided by the German Reich for a new armaments policy. A ship building tempo was set which was to extend for twenty years. This announcement was welcomed by capitalists and industrialists keen to exploit every opportunity; jobs would be created, trade and industry stimulated and suppliers' order books would be fattened to meet the demands of shipbuilding yards throughout Germany.

The new navy proved to be numerically inferior to Britain's by about fifty per cent but was superior in many other ways. German battleships had better guns, more modern firing control, better side armour protection, better optics, better shells, and better flash protection in the event of an enemy shell striking near the magazine. By contrast, the British battleships had some shortcomings in these areas. British shells were unreliable and often broke up on impact or failed to explode. It was observed at the Battle of Jutland in 1916 that some British shells thudded against the sides of German battleships and fell uselessly into the sea without exploding. Britain relied too much on the integrity of various armaments manufacturers to ensure quality control and reliability; explosive propellant for their shells was often unstable and weaker side armour was evident on their battleships. Flash protection to their powder magazines also was not up to German safety standards. A well-placed enemy shell hitting an unprotected magazine could have disastrous consequences and cause a ship to explode in a cataclysmic fire-ball; the problem was aggravated by the British habit of leaving their magazine doors open in order to speed the rate of fire in battle conditions. As early as January 1898, voices of concern were heard in London arguing that if Germany implemented her new naval plan it would upset the balance of power. Britain began to consider her own position and was forced into a programme of increasing her own naval strength; in effect the arms race between the two countries had begun.

By 1904, detailed plans of war operations against Germany were drawn up by the Admiralty. In that year, Sir John Arbuthnot Fisher became First Sea Lord of the Admiralty and as such the professional head of the Royal Navy. His motto was the three Rs – ruthless, relentless and remorseless. He was full of energy and determination and was to become Von Tirpitz's greatest opponent. He had the following comments to make at the Hague Peace Conference of 1899: '... *Hit your enemy in the belly, and kick him when he is down, and boil his prisoners in oil – if you take any – and torture his women and children. Then people will keep clear of you* ...' One wonders what he might have said at a war conference? Fisher was the man credited with revitalising the Royal Navy.

In 1911, Churchill was appointed First Lord of the Admiralty and thus became the political head of the Royal Navy. The Royal Navy had been the world's finest for hundreds of years and had a long tradition of great sea battles and numerous victories; Lord Nelson, after all, had defeated the combined navies of the French and Spanish at Trafalgar in 1805. Battle strategy was always about taking an offensive role and charging out to victory; it may have been this tradition of victory that caused naval architects and designers of British warships to overlook these elements of protection and thus leave their ships vulnerable under attack conditions. Britain had hoped for a great sea battle and a second Trafalgar by annihilating the German Navy, and confidently predicted that the war would end in a month. The Germans were aware of the fact that they were outnumbered by two to one in terms of battleships and had no intention of risking their fleet in an all-out confrontation; instead they considered wearing down the Royal Navy whenever the opportunity arose with sorties and skirmishes. The Germans took great pride in their Imperial Navy, to such an extent that the Kaiser was furious to learn that the armoured cruiser *Blücher* was lost as a result of Royal Navy action at the battle of the Dogger Bank in January 1915. The Kaiser promptly sacked his chief-of-staff, Von Ingenohl, for allowing the loss to occur and replaced him with Admiral Von Pohl in February 1915. All things considered, including their great land army, the Germans were also optimistic of an early victory by spring of 1915.

However as May 1915 dawned on the southern coast of Ireland, the Great War still seemed very remote from its inhabitants. For some, joining the British Army promised new career opportunities; for others it promised adventure and an escape from poverty at home. About 160,000 Irishmen responded to the call to enlist and signed up – 49,000 were killed while fighting for the British. Irish nationalists who joined for ideological reasons believed that their efforts in participation would prompt Britain to grant Home Rule to Ireland. Many believed the war would last only a month. However, other Irishmen fomented rebellion against Britain and colluded with Germany as they planned an event that culminated in the Easter Rising of 1916. Unionists pledged their full support and ironically welded very close bonds of friendship with their fellow nationalists as they fought a common enemy in the trenches of Europe.

Fishermen on the southern Irish coast got a first-hand glimpse of the war at sea as they toiled daily in their small fishing boats. They witnessed the sinking of merchant ships on a regular basis as they fell victim to torpedo or mine. The luckless victims and dripping survivors of these calamities were mainly non-nationals and deemed to belong to a faraway war. Coastal fishermen held submarines in great awe and trepidation and felt a great need to be ashore before darkness each evening in case one should be encountered. In the main, Germany was perceived as the nation that ravaged Belgium and slaughtered innocent neutrals in towns and cities on her way to war. As early as August 1914, some expressions of anti-German sentiment were evident; in particular the citizens of Cork city were incensed by the outrages perpetrated in Belgium. Prisoners who were seized from a captured German ship were marched through Cork and triggered an anti-German demonstration by their presence. Correspondents warned against the dangers of employing Germans or Austrians in the country and of complacency towards aliens and spies masquerading as musicians.

While Ireland adopted a neutral stance, this neutrality leaned heavily in favour of Britain and her Allies, as Germany was perceived to be the nation that started the war in the first place. Recruiting meetings were a regular occurrence in Cork city and often attended by large crowds, sometimes as many as 5,000 people. At these meetings, the horrors of war were not mentioned, but rather the danger to the country, the reasons for fighting and the ideals at stake. Some meetings were enlivened by the attendance of brass bands or the showing of magic-lantern war pictures. The romantic concept of war was yet to be shattered by the horrific meaningless slaughter at the Front.

However, the drab reality was slowly percolating home as grieving Irish mothers and wives received dreaded telegrams conveying the loss of their loved ones in the mud and barbed wire of the Western Front. The crippled and the maimed were also returning to stunned relatives. Some had been subjected to poison gas and were little better than invalids, their emaciated bodies racked by continuous coughing and congested lungs.

The concept of a distant war was suddenly shattered by a German U-boat attack and rapid sinking of the *Lusitania* on 7 May 1915, only twelve miles off the Old Head of Kinsale. The full savagery and horror of war was delivered to Ireland's doorstep with the mindless slaughter of 1,198 innocent civilians, including mothers with babes-in-arms. It seemed a diabolical barbarity that 2,000 non-combatants should be attacked without warning, that not even a minute's grace was allowed for the passengers and crew to take to the boats, that the murderous thrust was given in the full knowledge that it would mean the slaughter of hundreds of women and children and that this butchery was the act of a government which was, until recently, assumed to lead a civilised and humane nation. It was wrongly believed at the time that a second torpedo was discharged at the *Lusitania,* thereby reducing still further any chance of escape by her innocent passengers. Many people who saw the bodies of the *Lusitania* dead laid out in Queenstown (now named Cobh) over the next few days were filled with pity, horror and revulsion. Consternation was created among all classes on the southern Irish coast as the incident was strongly condemned and a greater determination to defeat Germany was proclaimed. On the day of the *Lusitania*'s departure from New York, the German Embassy issued a notice in the American press, warning passengers that vessels flying the British flag were liable for attack. This lent credence to the belief that the crime was premeditated and that the murderer expected to be acquitted of his foul deed for having warned his victim in advance of his intentions. To the people of southern Ireland, the apex of horror of the Great War had been reached. The world was shocked in 1912 by the loss of the *Titanic* to an iceberg, but the shock bore no parallel to that felt by the loss of the *Lusitania,* which was needlessly sacrificed to the insatiable gods of war.

2

Merchant Ships at War

THE DAWN OF WAR IN 1914 saw Britain as the world's foremost maritime nation with every reason to sing 'Britannia Rules the Waves'. Both her merchant ships and passenger liners dominated the seven seas and made up one-sixth of all shipping afloat. Britain's achievements over the centuries were largely due to her predominance as an ocean power. Her great Empire and Colonies were created by her merchant fleets and the navy that guarded them. Britain's Merchant Navy was established with a great tradition long before the Royal Navy was spawned.

In 1600, a consortium of London merchants founded the legendary English East India Company and were granted a royal charter to trade in the East Indies and Asia. From humble beginnings, the company grew to staggering proportions and traded for 270 years with such countries as India, Persia, Egypt, the Mollucas, Java, Siam, Borneo, Indonesia, Japan and ports on the China Sea. They dealt mainly in the importation of pepper, nutmeg, cloves, cinnamon and various spices as well as raw silk from China, Indian calico, cotton, sugar and saltpetre to make gunpowder. Many of their imported goods from the East were later re-exported from England to all parts of Europe, from ports on the Baltic to Venice on the Adriatic. Outward-bound East India ships were largely empty except for provisions and limited amounts of woollen goods, tin, lead, quicksilver, iron goods as well as substantial amounts of silver bullion and, to a lesser degree, gold bullion to pay for purchases abroad. By 1620 this energetic company had seventy-six ships and had established shipbuilding yards on the Thames at Deptford and Blackwall to build their own ships with a staff of 500 shipwrights. Ironworks, foundries and forges were also established at the Thames shipyards where the company's blacksmiths manufactured chains, anchors, nails and various implements. A multiplicity of buildings and warehouses surrounded the shipyards and incorporated sail-making lofts, cordage spinning sheds, and rope walks. Abattoirs were also attached where live cattle were slaughtered on the hoof and their flesh salted and pickled to provision the long voyages ahead. To man the fleet, 2,500 mariners were employed at sea, in addition to agents staffing their various and scattered trading stations in the East.

At this time the East India Company was London's biggest employer of labour and was granted permission by the government to mint its own currency. The East India Company was founded at a time when Britain was facing something of an oak crisis, due to rapid depletion of its forests in the latter half of the sixteenth century to meet the demands of shipbuilding and charcoal fuel making. Ireland, by contrast, had abundant forests of top quality oak awaiting exploitation. This natural resource attracted the East India Company to southern Ireland in 1610, where they established a 300-strong settlement at Dundaniel on the Bandon river, in County Cork. Several thousand acres of land were purchased or leased and tree felling commenced immediately. A shipbuilding dock was constructed and warehouses, sheds and forges were erected. Prime pieces of timber were felled for shipbuilding and lesser pieces were used to make barrel staves and charcoal. By 1613, two ships of 600 tons burden were built on the Bandon river and made sail for India and Java. Dams and weirs were constructed across the river and its tributary, the Brinny, and energy from the river was harnessed to drive waterwheels that powered an iron smelter near Dundaniel Castle.

However, after fifteen years, the settlement went into decline for lack of timber, when it was said that 'not a single stick was left standing'. The depletion of surrounding oak forests caused the company to abandon these shores and in 1641 their settlement was described as being 'old and decayed'.

Trading in the Indies was not all plain sailing for the London company of merchants. The cost of replacing ships was high as their hulls rapidly wore out in tropical waters. A sudden storm, an error of navigation, or a military engagement with the enemy could send a ship to the bottom with its precious homeward-bound cargo. Many of the company's servants in the Indies and Far East traded dishonestly on their own account, well out of reach of their superiors in London. Indian famines were a regular occurrence and had the effect of depressing trade greatly. A prolonged Indian famine, which endured for six years in the 1620s, almost drove the company to bankruptcy. Fierce commercial and political rivalry from Dutch and Portuguese interests forced the East India company to build forts and garrison them with soldiers at strategic locations throughout their realm. Of necessity, their ships of commerce also participated in wartime activity and the installation of cannon about their decks was standard practice. Ships have played this dual role since the curtain first rose on war at sea.

For hundreds of years British merchant ship owners were often obliged to defend their country against invasion. The British fleet that took on the mighty Spanish Armada in 1588 was made up of a core of merchant ships. The Indian Empire, the American Colonies, and many other British possessions around the world were founded by merchant shipping enterprise alone.

As the British Empire evolved, it was inevitable that there would be a separation between ships of commerce and ships of war. This led to specialisation and the need to build warships as a separate entity. The merchant navy, or Mercantile Marine, was said to have been the parent of the Royal Navy. Both were so closely knit that it was often difficult to separate their histories. This separation and specialisation did not in any way make the Mercantile Marine redundant in wartime. On the contrary, they were called upon to transport troops, to serve as auxiliary warships, hospital or munition ships.

During the Crimean War of 1853, the Cunard company responded to a strong British Government appeal for ships; they placed six of their best steamers, *Cambria*, *Niagara*, *Europa*, *Arabia*, *Andes* and *Alps* at the disposal of the British Government, later adding to these their newest acquisitions the *Jura* and *Etna*. Samuel Cunard was knighted for his patriotic gesture and thereby forged strong links with the British Government. The practice was invoked in recent times when, in 1982, Argentinian forces challenged Britain in the Falklands, liners like the *Queen Elizabeth 2* and *Canberra* were requisitioned for troop transportation and other duties.

At the commencement of hostilities in 1914, Britain's merchant ships assisted in mine sweeping, submarine chasing or were converted to Q ships. The Q ships, or mystery ships, were ships of commerce plucked from an assortment of tramp-steamers, fishing trawlers and sailing ships. Such ships were requisitioned from their owners in the early months of 1915 by the Admiralty for wartime use. After their civilian crews were paid off, these vessels were dispatched to Queenstown for conversion to decoys. The notation Q is derived from the name of their Irish base at Queenstown. Conversion often entailed name changing, adjustment of ships colours, adding a dummy funnel, altering deck houses and generally disguising the ship. The main objective was the installation of a gun about the ship and a means of concealing or disguising it by adopting various ruses.

The Queenstown authorities maintained a high state of security as they were ever conscious of Sinn Féin elements who might leak information to Germany. Sinn Féin, an Irish nationalist group, strove to seek independence from Britain, and were quick to realise that Britain's downfall might be Ireland's opportunity. Colluding with Germany was seen as a means to achieving their goals, and as potential German intelligence agents, they were ideally located.

Q ships were devised by Churchill as a means of countering the submarine menace. The vessels were intended to steam the high seas and entice U-boats to attack them in the belief that they were unarmed merchant ships which could safely be approached to bring them within torpedo range.

An approaching submarine might surface to challenge its victim, or it might first launch a torpedo and then surface to watch or identify the sinking ship. Either way a submarine on the surface was very vulnerable to single or multiple shots to the base of its conning tower from a concealed Q ship gun which was manned by trained gunners from the Royal Navy. To complete the deception, navy personnel on board the decoy vessel wore the plain and shabby clothing of civilian crews. Cargo hatches of Q ships were crammed with timber or sealed casks to afford additional buoyancy in the event of their hulls being ruptured by a torpedo. Their exploits as decoys called for great bravery combined with fighting skill, sound seamanship and a highly-developed imagination. As a result, their officers were hand picked.

An ideal captain would have the virtues of the cleverest angler, the most patient stalker, and the attributes of a cool and unperturbed seaman. Q ships sometimes patrolled the seas in vain for months on end, without encountering a single submarine. The boredom and suspense might suddenly be broken by shells whizzing from nowhere and exploding about the ship. In the distance, the low-lying enemy submarine might be seen firing its deck gun while keeping out of range of retaliation. At this point, the Q ship captain would be obliged to maintain the bluff of being in charge of an innocent merchant ship. This coolness would be maintained despite the possibility that some of his colleagues may be dying, or were dead, and his ship might be badly holed, sinking and on fire from the attack. The captain would patiently endure the nightmare in the hope that the attacking submarine would eventually get close enough for a knockout shot from the Q ship's concealed gun. To assist in the deception, the Q ship would launch its lifeboat with a party of sailors rowing away in apparent panic from their stricken ship to give the impression that it was abandoned.

To the eyes of an unsuspecting U-boat commander, the foundering ship appeared to be deserted and therefore safe for close examination or even boarding for inspection of its cargo. In reality, a hidden team of gunners remained on board in tense anticipation of the moment when they could drop their disguise and open fire on the unsuspecting U-boat. In practice, attacking submarines usually closed range from 500 to 800 yards before attacking the enemy. At this point the Q ship gunners would declare their hand by dropping the false side or unhinging the dummy lifeboat to bring their gun to bear on the submarine which now found itself in a very vulnerable position on the surface. In a simultaneous action, the Q ship would hoist the White Ensign on the ship's mast as they dispatched the submarine to a watery grave with a few well-placed shells. The appearance of a large oil slick on the surface was confirmation that the submarine's hull was ruptured and its occupants committed to the silent army of the dead at the bottom of the sea. A successful Q ship captain would be handsomely rewarded with a bonus of £1,000 to be divided at his own discretion amongst the crew.

Q ships, however, were not always victorious; sometimes their hulls were broken in half by an exploding torpedo and crew members would be obliged to abandon their ship for real. Such calamities often occurred several hundred miles west of Fastnet in the open Atlantic. Submarines adopted the strategy of lying back a distance from these drifting lifeboats in the hope of further attacking a rescue ship that might come to assist them. In many instances, the nearest rescue vessel might be several hundred miles distant and unaware of the plight of the survivors. Mist and rain as well as oncoming night were just some of the hardships to be endured by the drifting lifeboats and their helpless crews. Night was often followed by a hopeless dawn without the slightest glimmer of a passing ship or hope of rescue. Days of suspense and hopelessness became weeks; the downhearted crews suffered from cold, wet and fatigue. Their spirits might further be dampened at the sight of darkening skies as gales freshened from an ominous ocean. Some lifeboat occupants died of exposure and had to be heaved overboard and committed to the deep. Some became hysterical or mad; others died of their injuries or succumbed to the terrors of thirst and drank salt water with devastating consequences.

Such Q ship defeats or indecisive battles with submarines betrayed Churchill's decoy strategy to the Germans who were quick to report their close encounters to their superiors at Wilhelmshaven. U-boat commanders soon realised that it was safer to adopt a policy of shoot first and ask questions later. It was no longer safe to surface and challenge a suspect ship to establish if it was an enemy or neutral vessel.

Q ships were responsible for the sinking of at least twelve submarines but became largely ineffective when the Germans discovered their true nature. Not content with the Q ship strategy, Winston Churchill racked his brains to find other means of defeating the submarine menace. The depth charge had not yet been invented nor had the hydrophone as a listening device that could detect submarines as they lurked beneath the waves.

In February 1915, Churchill issued top secret orders to all merchant ships including the *Lusitania*: in future British merchant ships were urged to fly the flags of other nations to mislead the U-boats; if ordered by a submarine to halt, they were to attempt to ram that vessel at full speed and rupture its hull with their sharp prows; if not in a favourable position, they were to flee the scene at full speed and refuse the challenge of 'halt and search'. The Admiralty would again pay substantial cash rewards for success. Plans were also put in place to install a single gun on the aft deck of merchant ships to enable those ships to fire at pursuing submarines as they fled the scene. It took some time to implement this policy and it was approaching 1917 when the vast majority of merchant ships had their aft gun in place. The stated purpose of the gun was for defensive purposes only and gunned merchant ships were referred to as defensively armed merchant vessels or DAMVs. The late John Light believed that two such guns were erected on the aft deck of the *Lusitania* prior to her loss off Kinsale. To date nothing has been found to substantiate his claim.

In the early months of the war, German submarines observed Cruiser Rules when attacking enemy merchant shipping. These rules were in place for hundreds of years and observed by most civilised nations who found themselves embroiled in a war at sea. In essence, a warship or submarine could not attack, sink or capture an enemy merchant ship without first making provision for the safety of its civilian crew. In the case of a challenging submarine, merchant ship captains were given instructions to halt and abandon their ship or subject it to search for contraband cargo. The challenge was usually implemented by the submarine firing a single warning shot from its deck gun before announcing its intention. Where a ship was abandoned, the U-boat commander allowed ample time for the launching and boarding of the ship's lifeboats by their crew. Abandoning crews were urged to make full haste in rowing away from their ships which were subsequently torpedoed and sunk. U-boat commanders were especially nervous if crew members delayed in taking to the boats. Some ambushed merchant ships transmitted last-minute radio calls for help which were liable to bring speeding destroyers sweeping over the horizon to retaliate. To qualify for protection of life under Cruiser Rules, the challenged merchant ship was obliged to comply with certain stipulations; it could not use false colours by flying the flag of another country and thereby attempt to mislead; it could not act in a hostile manner such as attempting to ram or open fire with a gun, and it could not flee the scene once challenged. By flouting these guidelines, it would forfeit its right to protection under Cruiser Rules and would assume the status of a belligerent ship, and as such, be subject to destruction by the enemy without regard for the safety of life on board.

The advent of Q ships, the misuse of ships colours, and the hostile reaction of merchant ships in ramming submarines sounded the death knell for German chivalry in the war at sea. In effect, neutrals were stripped of any rights to protection under international law. Submarine commanders realised that it was no longer safe to appear on the surface and continued to fight the war beneath the waves. An American journalist of the time wryly commented that: *'Britannia not only ruled the waves but also waived the rules.'*

The effect of Churchill's new policies meant that all merchant ships including Q ships and neutrals were indistinguishable in view of the misuse of flags, a policy which caused massive loss of life and played havoc on the high seas.

3

The Majestic Era

THE WORD LINER IS derived from ships that travelled between fixed points, or lines, on a repetitive basis. The origins of passenger liners date back to the early 1800s, when wooden vessels known as packet ships made regular crossings on the Atlantic, from England to America with passengers, cargo and mail. These timber-built ships averaged between 400 and 1,000 tons in weight and were noted for their fat hulls and bulbous bows. By contrast their successors, the clipper ships, were designed with slim racing hulls and knife-edge prows to slice through the ocean. Packet ships incorporated attractive head rails and carved figure heads on their bowsprits with square transoms decorated with ornate carving scroll work. These flat-decked ships were three-masted with a single house or caboose between the masts. Another deck feature was a longboat lashed down with ropes to ring bolts. A galley was also incorporated where steerage passengers were obliged to cook their own food. Sleeping quarters were in dark, low-ceiling spaces below deck and sanitation was of the most rudimentary type, and almost non-existent during storm conditions. At the beginning of a voyage, the longboat was generally filled with crates of chickens and livestock, to stave off, for a while at least, the monotony of salted beef, pork and fish. A voyage could take anywhere from 35 to 80 days crossing from Europe to America.

In the years 1846–55 there was a tremendous surge in the emigrant trade as a result of the Irish famine and the actions of some landlords in evicting their starving tenants. These destitute hordes often faced starvation or emigration; most opted for the latter. Many emigrants also poured out of England to escape similar conditions. During the month of April 1853, for example, it is recorded that 27,000 people embarked on ships at Liverpool bound for America. Greedy and unscrupulous ship owners saw the opportunity for profit and exploitation as they made substandard and poorly-rigged ships available to the emigrant trade. Corrupt crews and manipulative captains were all too often evident. Between-deck areas were fitted out with sleeping stalls to utilise every possible space. The emigrant's trauma, on leaving family and loved ones, was exacerbated by torturous waiting on docks for days on end in all conditions of weather, as the ship owner delayed sailing schedules to cram in yet more passengers.

Government regulations were flouted at every turn as ships were overcrowded in the interest of maximising profit. Ship food for the emigrants was scant to say the least, and consisted mainly of Indian corn or yellow meal. Packet ship crews were recruited from the riff-raff of waterfront dives and aptly referred to as 'packet rats'. Emigrants were routinely cheated, robbed, beaten and degraded during a voyage of appalling terror and fear. Conditions of overcrowding, squalor, lack of sanitation and general starvation proved a perfect breeding-ground for such diseases as typhus, dysentery, cholera and smallpox. On average, one sixth of a ship's complement died of one or more of these various diseases, either during the trip or in quarantine after they reached their destination. Those who died on the ship were unceremoniously heaved overboard without recourse to last rites or spiritual consolation. An emigrant ship named the *Virginus* set out with 476 passengers from Liverpool in 1847 and lost 158 during the voyage. Their deaths were attributed to fever and dysentery; these ships earned themselves the nickname of coffin ships as their occupants died like flies. Those who survived the terror of the voyage had to endure lice and scabies as well as seasickness; the agonising misery of wet dingy holds was accompanied by the overpowering stench of excreta and vomit. During storms, passengers were kept below decks and often deprived of food for days on end.

Between 1847–53, fifty-nine emigrant ships foundered. These unseaworthy hulks fell prey to the savage moods of the Atlantic when they were tossed around like corks, in full-blown storms and driving rain. The terror felt by the emigrants was multiplied beyond belief when bedding became wet and sodden as mountainous seas broke over leaky deck-planking to drench the unfortunate emigrants beneath. Fine weather would offer some respite as the weary travellers were allowed up on deck from the shivering cold below. As their ship bore north, they encountered freezing fog and icebergs to add further variations to their misery.

The march of science and technology greatly improved the lot of the emigrants with the introduction of the steamship and the development of the iron hull in place of vulnerable timber ships. This new breed of ship was driven by engine and propeller and was no longer dependent on the vagaries of wind and billowing canvas. These early steamships gave little consideration to passenger comfort other than safeguarding them from the worst conditions of wind and weather. As time wore on, however, competing shipping lines began to entice passengers by offering heating, running water, cooked food served by stewards, and even carpets on their ships. Seasickness was never mentioned, but as ships embarked on a voyage their carpets were routinely rolled up and stored throughout the crossing. The passenger liner began to evolve rapidly from the 1870s onwards, with ever greater and faster ships being built by Britain, France and Germany.

By the turn of the century, Atlantic crossings could be made in six to seven days and with the advent of the *Lusitania,* the crossing time was reduced to less than five days. The prestigious Blue Riband, or speed record, was firmly in Britain's hands. British yards had even built some of the earlier German liners and merchant ships. However, by 1890, the Germans decided to lay down a series of great liners that would dominate the Atlantic and gain commercial supremacy over a Britain which was beginning to buckle under the challenge.

The final years leading up to 1900 saw Britain's pre-eminence of the North Atlantic begin to wane. In 1897, Germany swept the Blue Riband from Britain when it launched the new record-breaking ship, the *Kaiser Wilhelm der Grosse,* which weighed 14,000 tons and achieved a speed of twenty-two knots. This ship became the largest and fastest liner in the world and gave the German people immense pride and satisfaction. People were awestruck by her four towering funnels which were staggered in pairs to accommodate the first class dining-room within, unimpeded by boiler uptakes. Apart from the *Great Eastern,* no other Atlantic liner possessed so many funnels and the public soon equated more funnels with more luxury and more speed. This unique funnel arrangement was adapted on the four subsequent German liners. Ship builders were only too glad to pander to the whims of the public and often fitted a fourth dummy funnel to enhance the prestige of their liners. Even ships as large as the *Titanic* resorted to the dummy funnel ruse to attract the travelling public.

The loss of the speed record in 1897 was a severe blow to Britain's pride, especially as it occurred when the diamond jubilee of Queen Victoria was being celebrated. In 1900, the Hamburg-America line (HAPAG) of Germany eclipsed the *Kaiser Wilhelm der Grosse* by launching their record-breaking ship *Deutschland.* Other great German liners followed in rapid succession, such as the *Kaiser Wilhelm II,* named after the Imperial German Emperor, the *Kronprinz Wilhelm,* after his son, and the *Kronprinzessin Cecilie,* after the Crown Prince's wife. During the construction of these beautiful liners, provision had been made in each case for their future conversion to AMCs or armed merchant cruisers. This decision may have been inspired by an event that occurred in happier times when the Kaiser was on good terms with his grandmother Queen Victoria and his uncle, Prince Edward. In August 1889, a reluctant Prince of Wales invited his insufferable nephew, the young Kaiser, to attend the Royal Navy review at Spithead in England. The Kaiser was even made an honorary Admiral of the

Fleet and wore an admiral's uniform for the event. He was shown around various warships and torpedo boats but seemed especially interested in the newly launched *Teutonic*. The Kaiser wandered about this White Star liner for two hours and noted that various guns were erected around the ship's decks and there was armour plating on her hull. She was stated to be ready for war.

The recently built royal family of German liners was faster, bigger, and more modern than any of Britain's best. As a result they captured much business from their ailing competitors. They were built to a high standard of strength and quality, which was to stand them in good stead in later years when they found themselves embroiled in the First World War. German liners were famous for their brass bands which always played, irrespective of weather or Atlantic storm. The era of the four-funnel liner was surely born with the advent of these ocean greyhounds. In total, only fourteen would ever be built between such countries as France, Britain, and Germany. It was felt that the apex of marine technology and architecture had been achieved with these majestic giants, which were owned by such companies as the British Cunard Company, the American White Star Line, Hamburg-America, Norddeutscher Lloyd, Union Castle and Compagnie Générale Transatlantique of France.

At the outbreak of hostilities, the *Kaiser Wilhelm der Grosse* was requisitioned for war service by the German Navy. Eight guns were installed on her decks and she assumed the role of armed merchant cruiser. Her career as a marauder proved to be very brief when, having sunk some minor ships, she was trapped by HMS *Highflyer* while taking on board coal on the coast of West Sahara on what were then Spanish colonial waters. The captain of the *Highflyer* challenged his opponent to surrender, only to be told that Germans do not surrender. Both ships opened fire and the *Kaiser Wilhelm der Grosse* eventually foundered and sank on 26 August 1914, an ignominious end to a great ship. Her wreck is still marked on current sea charts of the area.

In 1902, Britain decided that something must be done to curb these 'German upstarts' and restore Britain's pride. This was to take all of ten years to achieve. Planning began for two new British ships that were to be the largest, fastest, and most luxurious the world had ever known. They were to be half as big again as anything afloat and had engines three-quarters greater in horse power to achieve record-breaking speeds. Their designers were at the cutting edge of science and technology in pioneering the use of enormous steam turbines to drive the ship. This was a leap toward the future and abandonment of well-tried and tested, but less efficient, reciprocating engines. It would also be the first time that an arrangement of four propellers would be used on a liner. The *Kaiser Wilhelm der Grosse* had only two propellers. The bunkers on the new Cunarders would carry 7,000

During construction, thousands of workers daily swarmed aboard the *Lusitania* in the course of fitting out her hull and machinery at John Brown's shipyard in Glasgow.

tons of coal to fuel the insatiable appetites of twenty-four boilers. This was more than double the amount of boilers on the *Kaiser Wilhelm der Grosse*.

It was decided to adopt the old Roman name of the province of Portugal in christening one of these twins *Lusitania,* while her sister would be named *Mauretania* after an old Roman province in Africa. The superiority and speed of these ships was such that it would be all of twenty-one years before they could be challenged. This challenge came from the Germans in July 1929 when they launched the new record-breaker, the *Bremen,* and captured the Blue Riband once more from the British.

The *Lusitania* was built in John Brown's yard on Clydebank while her sister, the *Mauretania,* was built in Swan Hunter's at Tyneside. The British Government made available the entire cost of the two ships in the form of a loan of over £2.5 million in addition to an annual subsidy to defray running costs. This staggering sum of money was to be repaid at a modest rate of interest over the following twenty years. Payments would not fall due until the ships were launched and selling passenger fares to cross the Atlantic Ocean.

However, certain admiralty stipulations had to be complied with. In the main, these referred to the design of the hull and machinery. All vital machinery was to be installed below the waterline, this was to afford protection from shellfire in wartime. The ships would be available for naval service, at a moment's

As thousands of onlookers crowd the riverbank, the newly launched *Lusitania* steams down the Clyde on her way to the open sea.

notice, in times of national emergency. Provision would be made during construction to allow for the installation of twelve 6-inch quick-firing guns on her decks, as well as converting certain compartments to magazines for storing shells. A speed of twenty-five knots had to be achieved; failure to do so would result in penalties in the form of reductions in annual government subsidies. The Cunard company had to remain British and not slip into foreign hands, especially those of John Pierpont Morgan, the American multimillionaire and corporate raider who had recently purchased the White Star line in 1902.

The *Lusitania* had four cavernous boiler rooms which included twenty-
boilers: these boilers were sub-divided into 192 fire grates which consumed
insatiable 1,000 tons of coal per day.

While the designers of the *Lusitania* looked to the future in planning great engines and machinery, the architects looked to the past in planning her decor. Public rooms on the *Lusitania* were treated in Italian and French renaissance styles. The grand staircase was in the fifteenth-century Italian model. There were Adams, Sheraton, and Chippendale state rooms. The grand dining saloon was based on the Petit Trianon at the Palace of Versailles. One writer stated that the stately homes of England had gone to sea in the form of these beautiful ships. Walls were panelled in highly polished mahogany and walnut; floors were covered with luxurious carpets and windows were richly curtained. Numerous settees and sofas were covered in silk, and enormous marble fireplaces led up to beautifully plastered ceilings by Italian masters. Stained glass skylights allowed natural daylight to enter from above to highlight the artist's creation.

Following the conventions of the day, passengers were divided into three classes, each catering for a different segment of the travelling public. These classes were segregated, necessitating triplicate smoking rooms, lounges, dining saloons and promenade areas. Classes were not allowed to mix and it was considered improper to do so. First class on the *Lusitania* drew a travelling elite, captains of industry, diplomats, filmstars, opera singers and royalty. It was said that a millionaire could travel on the *Lusitania* without having to mix with someone who was not also a

The first class smoking lounge was luxuriously appointed. Ladies were not allowed to enter and those who wished to smoke were obliged to use their stateroom.

millionaire. Regal suites and en suite rooms on the *Lusitania* incorporated a bedroom, sitting room, and private bathroom as well as telephone and hot and cold running water. The bulk of third class was mostly made up of emigrants who were accommodated in the most undulating part of the ship, namely the bow. Food for the emigrant class was prepared in the same galley as that used to feed the crew, and was said to be quite wholesome. The designers realised that the vast majority of third class passengers would never have seen a flush toilet before and might have some difficulty understanding the principles involved. To prevent confusion, it was decided to fit self-flushing toilets that flushed continuously while the occupant remained seated. Third class cabins, depending on size, were either two, four or six berth. Cunard were obliged to emboss their company emblem on the bedclothes to discourage pilferage at the end of the voyage. Second class was targeted at the professional and middle classes and said to be as luxurious as first class on earlier liners. The second class area of the ship was located mainly over the enormous 68,000 HP engines and aft of number four funnel; this area suffered excessive vibration and jarring and was gutted shortly after its trials in 1907. Additional stiffening, buttressing and reinforcing was introduced to alleviate the problem. Throughout the *Lusitania*'s career, this area was plagued by vibration which had been reduced but never eliminated; Cunard played down this unpleasant trait.

Apart from passengers the *Lusitania* also provided accommodation for its own 850 staff; accommodation for stewardesses and matrons was safely located in the middle of the first class accommodation area. This made visits by male crew members impossible; those who attempted to make secret visits were promptly sacked when caught. Cunard also provided doctors and free medical care aboard the *Lusitania*. A special twenty-four bed hospital was located on the shelter deck and subdivided into four wards; in addition a special isolation ward to cope with infectious diseases was located in the stern of the ship. Some expectant mothers planned their deliveries to coincide with their emigration, thereby taking advantage of the free maternity service provided.

Cavernous kitchens were also provided to cater for the preparation of up to 10,000 meals per day. These were supported by numerous pantries, bakeries, food stores and refrigerated compartments which were used to store such provisions as fish, dairy produce, vegetables and fruit, beef, mutton, poultry, ice, beer and wines. Some compartments were fitted with rails and hooks on which to hang meat. Provisions such as potatoes and flour were taken on board by the ton. Such exotic dishes as lobster, oyster, turtle, partridge, quail, grouse, pheasant and Bordeaux pigeons graced the first class menu; food was said to be of better quality than any of the best hotels in Europe.

The architect of the *Lusitania,* Leonard Peskett, had the difficult task of serving two masters; the

The magnificent barrel-vaulted ceiling in the first class lounge was sub-divided into twelve stained-glass panels depicting the twelve months of the year. Panels were captioned in different languages. Each end of this great room was adorned with a 14-foot-high green marble fireplace; walls were panelled in highly polished mahogany and walnut. The beautiful plaster work on the ceilings was painted in ivory to offset the room's green carpets and upholstery; the lounge was said to have created an atmosphere of quiet repose.

exacting demands of the Admiralty had to be met in placing all vital machinery below the waterline, while at the same time also meeting Cunard's requirements in providing for over 2,000 passengers and 850 crew. To meet these criteria, Peskett was forced to build a high ship with six decks above the waterline. The sleek and slim appearance of the *Lusitania* earned her the nickname of the 'Greyhound of the Seas'. When the *Lusitania* was launched, she was the largest man-made floating object in the world, and the envy of every other maritime nation as she easily achieved her record-breaking speed of twenty-five knots and returned the Blue Riband to British hands once more. Britain's immense pride in the stunning technological achievements of the newly launched *Lusitania* was shared by her Irish neighbours, who could justifiably claim to have made a contribution to her speed by the liner's incorporation of powerful turbine engines. Charles Parsons, the Irish inventor of the turbine engine, was born in 1854 and was one of the six sons of the third Earl of Rosse. His descendants still reside at the ancient family demesne of Birr Castle in Ireland. In 1894, Parsons formed the Marine Steam Turbine Company and took out a patent on his new invention; in August of the same year, his company built the world's first turbine driven ship, *Turbinia*, at Wallsend. In trials carried out in 1897, the *Turbinia* achieved 34.5 knots and staged a spectacular display of her speed at Queen Victoria's Diamond Jubilee Fleet

The book case in the ship's library was 26 feet long by 9 feet high and made of mahogany with glass doors; the reading desks with a central reading lamp were also made of mahogany. Walls were panelled in grey and cream silk brocade; ceilings and walls were cream coloured to complement the rose carpet, and two large white marble fireplaces burned coal fires to create a homely effect. A magnificent stained-glass dome allowed natural daylight to enter the library.

Review in Spithead. In 1911, the Order of Merit was bestowed on Sir Charles Parsons for his contribution to science. The tiny pioneer ship, *Turbinia,* can be seen at the Newcastle Discovery Museum.

When the Great War was declared in 1914, Cunard had twenty-six vessels in commission apart from tugs, lighters and other subsidiaries. In keeping with a 1903 agreement between Britain and Cunard, it was agreed that her entire fleet would be at the disposal of the Admiralty for wartime duty. The following passenger liners were commandeered for combat purposes: *Aquitania, Caronia, Laconia, Campania* and *Carmania.* Some were converted to seaplane carriers; aeroplanes could take off from these ships but could not land on deck and were later retrieved from the sea. The aircraft-carrier was still in the future and only a vision in the minds of naval engineers. The *Aquitania* and *Caronia* were fully dismantled and fitted out as armed merchant cruisers in the first days of August 1914. This Herculean task was carried out by a team of no less than 5,000 men who completed the work in only six days. It meant the ruthless stripping out of all their luxurious fittings and splendid furniture; these items were carefully stored ashore for future use in peacetime. More than 2,000 wagon loads of fittings were taken ashore from the two liners. A third ship, the *Carmania,* arrived in port to be similarly converted.

The *Aquitania,* which had been first launched on 21 April 1913, was a third and even bigger four-funnel liner than her older twin sisters the *Lusitania* and *Mauretania*. Her conversion had already been completed on 7 August when she had larger 6-inch guns installed on her deck; on that day she hoisted the White Ensign and officially became HMS *Aquitania*. On a foggy morning in late August, the *Aquitania* sighted the Leyland liner *Canadian* and ordered it to stop. As she approached the much smaller steamer, the master and watchkeepers lost sight of her under the bows with the result that the liner inadvertently rammed the *Canadian*. After assessing the damage to her bow, the *Aquitania* returned to Liverpool on 24 August 1914. The subsequent court of enquiry concluded that she was not suited for this type of duty and recommended that she be withdrawn from cruiser work. On 2 September, her ammunition and guns were removed and all her naval staff left the ship as it was returned to Cunard.

As a result of the collision with the *Canadian*, Cunard modified the *Aquitania* by building a new wheel house directly above the original, giving a far better view ahead. The *Aquitania* again entered government service on 11 May 1915, when she was hired to transport troops to the Dardanelles. She was painted in dazzle patterns to confuse the enemy. During the next few months she would transport 30,000 troops. The disastrous collapse of the Dardanelles campaign saw the *Aquitania* converted into a hospital ship and by early 1916 she had ferried 25,000 troops back home. In keeping with her hospital role, she was repainted to the internationally accepted hospital-ship colour scheme of white hull and broad green band around the hull punctuated by red crosses. Throughout most of 1916, the liner mainly assumed a standby role with only brief stints of hospital work to Malta and Alexandria before being laid up for the entire year of 1917. In March 1918, she was put back into service and played a vital role in transporting troops from America to Europe. The *Aquitania* had the unique distinction of having served in both wars. She had sailed 3 million miles and completed 884 Atlantic crossings and was sadly committed to the breaker's yard in 1949 after thirty-five years of gallant service. As she made her final melancholy voyage, she had the distinction of being the oldest and last four-funnel liner to ply the Atlantic Ocean.

The *Carmania* docked at Liverpool on 7 August 1914 and disembarked her passengers and crew to make way for the workforce waiting to modify the ship. Teams of painters set about disguising the funnels by applying black paint over the familiar Cunard red. Shipwrights cut out the bulwarks fore and aft on 'B' deck to provide for the installation of guns. Armour plating was installed over vulnerable parts of the ship. All woodwork in passenger quarters was taken away. Two of her holds were fitted with platforms, and magazines were fitted on them to accommodate shells. As a precaution, a system of magazine flooding was also installed to deal with fires. Speaking tubes and telephone systems were installed to provide communication for eight 4.7-inch calibre guns installed on her decks; these guns had a range of 9,000 yards. Two searchlights were installed, including a range finder for the guns, and extra protection was added to the coal bunkers. Ammunition was immediately taken aboard and stored in the magazines, together with a limited number of small arms in addition to rifles for the marines. The *Carmania* was back at sea on 14 August as a fully-fledged warship, and proceeded in a southerly direction across the Atlantic. She was soon to earn distinction for being the only British armed liner to sink a German armed liner in a shoot-out off the coast of Brazil.

Meanwhile the magnificent three-funnel German liner, *Cap Trafalgar,* found herself in Montevideo laden with passengers on the eve of war. This luxury liner was the finest ship of the Hamburg-South America line and was practically new, having made only one previous voyage. Unlike the oncoming *Carmania,* the German liner was not fitted with guns or equipped with munitions. On hearing that war had broken out, her captain, Langerhanz, took the precaution of disembarking all his passengers before setting course in an easterly direction to rendezvous with another German ship, the *Eber.* When both vessels met on the high seas, the *Eber* transferred armaments said to consist of ten guns and assorted ammunition to the *Cap Trafalgar*. As the liner's crew busied themselves installing the guns about the upper decks of the ship, Captain Langerhanz set course for the remote rocky island of Trinidade to keep a second appointment with three German colliers to replenish his coal bunkers.

However, his plans were interrupted by the appearance of the *Carmania* on the horizon. Both ships closed distance, and an inevitable sea-battle commenced immediately; guns blazed with both sides easily hitting their enormous targets. The German gunners concentrated their fire on the bridge of the *Carmania* and shell damage eventually carried away all the control gear, severing all telephone and range communication to her gunners. Fires broke out on both ships as exploding shells rained down on all sides. The *Carmania* gunners on the other hand concentrated on shelling the *Cap Trafalgar* near the waterline, eventually causing the ship to take water rapidly. The *Carmania*'s masts, ventilators, boats, and derricks were shot away as fire raged out of control on her decks. Fire hosepipes were disabled and shot away and as a result no water was available to tackle the fire; crew members had to rely on water buckets passed from hand to hand by bucket gangs in most appalling conditions of smoke and flames.

In the sweltering heat of the autumn battle fought out on the *Carmania,* immaculately dressed stewards in white uniforms served iced drinks, in tall glasses from silver trays, to the weary gunners. Meanwhile, below decks, the ship's doctor and his assistant were about to perform an amputation on a wounded gunner when a German shell whizzed through the room severing a piece of the operating table before embedding itself in the ship's main pillow store, whereupon the shell exploded creating a blinding snowstorm of feathers and causing the doctor to lose his patient for several terrifying minutes.

As the savage duel wore on, both ships suffered appalling damage. Luxurious saloons and deluxe suites were reduced to smouldering rubble. The once beautiful German liner boasted a magnificent winter garden with lofty palms and over a hundred potted plants. This one-time haven of tranquillity was now a blazing forest fire, ignited by bursting shells, as the thick brown smoke from the burning palms increased the misery of the already exhausted gunners. As fire ravaged the *Cap Trafalgar*, it was obvious to all that she would soon disappear beneath the waves. In the frenzy of battle her guns suddenly fell silent, and frantic efforts were made to launch her lifeboats. As the occupants pulled away from the inferno, the *Cap Trafalgar* rolled over on her beam end and sank.

The badly mauled *Carmania* limped back to Gibraltar over the next nine days, and entered a shipyard where she was refitted over several months. She was finally restored to liner service with the Cunard company in 1916.

The *Lusitania* and *Mauretania* were also recalled for conversion on the eve of the Great War. Careful plans were made to install twelve 6-inch quick-firing guns on their decks plus the usual magazine conversions. However, at a last-minute meeting, both ships were rejected from the list as it was deemed that their enormous coal consumption would outweigh their value as auxiliary cruisers. The *Lusitania*'s twelve gun rings were already in place in anticipation of the conversion that never took place. These rings were visible on her decks despite being planked over for her peacetime duties. She was ordered to return to her intended function of Atlantic ferry. The *Lusitania*, which had made 101 Atlantic crossings, was sent to her doom twelve miles off the Old Head of Kinsale when she fell victim to a German torpedo in May 1915.

The *Mauretania* was mostly engaged in troop transporting and hospital duty during the First World War. For this purpose she was painted in wartime dazzle paint to help confuse German submarines. After the war, she returned to her peacetime role as a North Atlantic ferry. She was duly converted to oil burning which eliminated all the backbreaking drudgery and grime of coaling her boilers, and also reduced her engine-room staff from over 300 people to 60. After a long and glorious career, she left New York for the last time on 26 September 1934 to a mournful farewell as she headed for the breaker's yard and destruction. Many other Cunard liners such the *Ausonia*, *Alunia*,

Ascania, *Andania*, and *Franconia* serving in the war were not so lucky and fell victim to torpedo and mine.

Another member of the four-funnel club, White Star, warrants a mention here. The White Star Line had produced some of the most famous steamers ever seen on the North Atlantic service. Innovation was a part of White Star's strategy and they concentrated on passenger comfort and size, while leaving expensive speed to Germany and Cunard. The launch of the *Lusitania* and *Mauretania* forced White Star to re-think its future strategy. It was decided to build a trio of great liners which would become the biggest in the world. The first two, *Olympic* and *Titanic*, would be built side by side at Harland and Wolff's shipyard in Belfast and once a vacant berth could be created, a third sister, the *Britannic* would be constructed. Neither thought nor money would be spared in the pursuit of excellence. This trio of superliners would each weigh 45,000 tons and be 900 feet long.

The first to be completed and launched was the *Olympic* in 1910. She was subsequently requisitioned for wartime as a troop transport and made four deliveries of troops to the Dardanelles. Later, in 1916, she was converted to a warship and fitted with 6-inch guns and re-painted in dazzle colours. She was a lucky ship and escaped various encounters and near misses from submarines. On one occasion, a German torpedo struck her but failed to explode. On 12 May 1918, she was loaded to the gunwales with American troops when her captain sighted a German submarine off the bow and took an immediate decision to ram it. While swinging into position, the *Olympic* opened fire with her forward gun as the submarine attempted to flee. However, the charging *Olympic* crashed into the submarine tearing a gigantic hole in its side and sending it plunging to the bottom. The submarine's captain, Rücker, amazingly survived the assault. The *Olympic* suffered considerable damage to her bow which was said to be misaligned by over 8 feet and had to enter a dockyard for repairs.

In October 1935, the *Olympic* ended a long and illustrious career as she made her last voyage to the scrapyard. When she made her final departure from Southampton with a skeleton crew, thousands lined the dockside to bid her a sad farewell.

Her unlucky sister, the *Titanic*, became the world's most famous shipwreck after striking an iceberg and sinking on her maiden voyage to America. The last of the trio, the *Britannic,* was being fitted out at the Belfast shipyard when war broke out. She never fulfilled her role as a passenger ferry and was requisitioned by the Admiralty for use as a hospital ship in November 1915. For her hospital duty she was painted white with two large red crosses and the international green band on her hull.

By now the campaign against the Turks was faltering and large scale evacuation of the wounded was necessary. November 1916 found the *Britannic* off the Greek coast on her sixth outbound trip. She was scheduled to collect 3,000 injured and wounded soldiers at Moúdhros. Before she made port, however, she was rocked by an explosion said to have been caused by a German mine, and shortly afterwards she rolled over and sank in several hundred feet of water.

The notion of arming passenger liners by both British and German governments was ill-conceived from the outset. These high-speed giants had insatiable appetites for coal and would prove extremely difficult to fuel on the high seas; their fragile non-armoured hulls would be vulnerable to enemy shells. Any success they hoped to achieve was far outweighed by their enormous cost and limited effectiveness; in essence both governments had inadvertently subsidised fleets of white elephants.

Time has not dimmed the public fascination for these once proud liners. In recent years, the *Lusitania, Titanic* and *Britannic* have all been located and recorded on camera by diver or remotely operated vehicle (ROV) while *Titanic* broke box-office records with James Cameron's masterpiece of cinema.

All three liners have been extensively surveyed by underwater craft. Their once grandiose staterooms and saloons are now inhabited by lowly fish. Decay and age have reduced their beautiful hulls to veritable scrapheaps; their great engines are silent in their tombs of perpetual darkness and their once gleaming white superstructures and colourful funnels have assumed the autumnal tones of rusty steel. Their roaring furnaces are extinguished and their cold grates are blanketed in silt. They will never complete their voyages, or excite the imagination of an awestruck public who crowded their berths to welcome them. Their lifeless hulks repose on a bleak landscape, sad monuments to the majestic era of bygone days.

4

A Damned Un-English Weapon

IN 1914 THE SUBMARINE was a new, untried weapon of war. The German name for these under-sea vessels was *Unterseeboot* hence the name U-boat. Admiral Von Tirpitz, the father of the German Navy, had stated in the Reichstag in 1901 that Germany had no need of submarines. With much prejudice abounding within the *Admiralstab,* the Germans were late to join the submarine club, and legend has it that they built their first U-boat in 1906 when every other major navy in the world (including the Portuguese and Turkish) had already added these underwater vessels to their fleets.

The British regarded the deployment of the U-boats as 'damned un-English'. It was not cricket to hide underwater in a sealed tin can and fight a sea battle. The true potential of these lowly-rated craft was not realised or debated in pre-war times and they were given scant consideration by both British and German admiralties. Trouble in the war at sea was expected to come from big guns mounted on surface battleships or converted liners. After all, the torpedo and the mine were still in the developmental stages and notoriously unreliable.

As the war unfolded between 1914 and 1918, Britain paid dearly for its disregard of the U-boat's potential for destruction. At the commencement of hostilities Germany had only a handful of small U-boats which were intended to provide back-up support to their navy in home waters. However, it was the humble, lowly-regarded U-boat that brought Imperial Germany to the threshold of victory with a campaign that sent over 11 million tons of Allied shipping to the bottom of the sea as well as inflicting damage to another 7 million tons. Germany achieved all this at the loss of 178 U-boats and 5,300 officers and men. The German high command were obsessed by their surface navy and despised their counterparts in the submarine service. It was not until the festivities of Kiel week in June 1914, when the Kaiser boarded and inspected the despised submarines, that their crews could feel any outward pride in their chosen profession. The Kaiser was obviously impressed by what he saw.

Life on board the submarine was anything but pleasant; conditions were cramped and stuffy. Atlantic storms tossed these slender craft around like corks, and crew members sometimes found themselves as much at war with nature as with the enemy. Winter in northern waters often produced bone-chilling temperatures of around 4 °C within the submarine, causing steel walls to be draped in beads of condensation which regularly fell in droplets on cold, exhausted bodies. These droplets were especially annoying to crew members who tried to snatch sleep in their cramped bunks or hammocks. When the opportunity arose, chilled submariners would make their way to the engine room to heat their numbed hands on the motors. To cope with their damp, cold environment, personnel were issued with leather clothing and warm woollen underclothing.

Due to the limited endurance of electric motors and their batteries, submarines were compelled to run a great deal on the surface. In this mode they could make much better progress by travelling on their diesel engines while simultaneously charging their batteries and flushing out foul air. In rough weather, travelling on the surface was most uncomfortable as the slender craft pitched and rolled in heavy seas causing waves to cascade down through the open conning-tower hatch to drench the squalid accommodation below decks. As this water slopped around the control area, it would inevitably enter the bilges which were already contaminated by spilled diesel, food scraps and vomit from seasick sailors.

The all-pervading smell of diesel fuel hung every-where and stuck to men's clothing even when ashore.

However, this was only one of many smells: unwashed bodies in unchanged clothing; spilled cooking fat from the galley, and the unsanitary and reeking restrooms, all heightened the stench. Submarine toilets were not the simple devices we daily take for granted in our homes. One needed some expertise in plumbing to understand their complexities. Flushing was achieved by operating a series of valves and levers which discharged the contents, by a burst of compressed air, to the outside world. It was not safe to flush these toilets when hiding in enemy waters by daylight, as the operation released a tell-tale burst of air bubbles to the surface which might betray the submarine's presence. Toilet traffic over the course of a long day submerged might cause pans to reach overflowing levels until cover of darkness would once more permit flushing or, in submarine parlance, 'blowing the head'. Unlucky trainee submariners sometimes erred in operating the complex valve system and might finish up covered from head to foot in the toilet's contents. Mercifully, the human nose numbs and becomes desensitised from exposure to continuous stench, and some relief was thereby afforded the senses of the crammed occupants. Washing and personal hygiene were non-existent and sailors had to depend on bathing in the sea when it was safe to do so. The chilly waters of the north Atlantic were not very enticing to bathers, causing many to forego what might be their first opportunity to wash in a period of seven to ten days.

In the warmer temperatures of Mediterranean waters, washing was an agreeable chore. Non-swimmers were attached to lines as they wallowed about the hull of the submarine. Summer patrolling in warmer climes contrasted sharply with conditions in the North Atlantic, and in these conditions submariners were forced to endure stifling heat in their sealed tin cans and fetid atmosphere. Sometimes enemy presence forced submarines to remain underwater for long periods thus causing life-threatening foul air and gasses to accumulate. Another occupational hazard was acid-burns from spills and overflows of large banks of storage batteries required for submerged running by electric motors. Discharging batteries generated inflammable hydrogen gas which was drawn off by the ventilating system; failure of the ventilation system and a single spark could trigger a hydrogen explosion, a catastrophe that befell many German submarines. A submariner's greatest fear, however, was deadly chlorine gas which was easily generated when leaking sea water came in contact with sulphuric acid in the batteries. Life aboard the submarine was a continuous cycle of foul air and dangerous gases, when submerged, and sodden misery when travelling on the surface. This was the life chosen by Lieutenant Commander Schwieger who was to earn notoriety by sinking the *Lusitania*.

Some U-boat commanders were described as decent men doing a dirty job, while others were regarded as cold-blooded killers and sadists. The U-boat continued to suffer bad press until 22 September 1914. On that day, Lieutenant Commander Otto Weddigen was on patrol off the Dutch coast in his primitive submarine U-9. In the space of little over an hour, he successfully stalked, torpedoed and sank three 12,000-ton British armoured warships: the *Hogue*, *Cressy* and *Aboukir* with a loss of 1,500 British servicemen's lives including many cadets just out of college. Weddigen returned home to a rapturous welcome; Germany went wild with the news and the Kaiser personally decorated Weddigen with the Iron Cross First and Second Class. The British Admiralty were shocked and stunned, and refused to accept that Weddigen could have achieved such results on his own. They claimed that several submarines were sighted at the time of battle and derided Weddigen's skill and courage. The method of attack by the U-boat was seen as unfair, and Roger Keyes, the Commodore of the British submarine service, scornfully compared it with a big game hunter stalking a tame elephant while it was chained to a tree. Later that year, on 15 October, Weddigen struck another numbing blow when he sank the Royal Navy cruiser *Hawke* off Aberdeen. Once more, loss of life was heavy and over 500 officers and men were drowned.

One thing was now certain: naval warfare would never be the same again. At last, both Royal and German Navies were compelled to take the submarine seriously. Weddigen's dazzling victory gave new impetus to the U-boat campaign, as submarines began to stalk Royal Navy warships openly, in broad daylight, off the English coast in a war of attrition. Each day they encountered hundreds of merchant ships plying their trade. It had not yet dawned on Germany that Britain's trade routes and supply ships were its greatest strength, as her commercial ships were allowed to proceed unmolested in spite of their vulnerability to attack.

The British Admiralty had formed their strategy for dealing with Germany long before war broke out. The Royal Navy was preoccupied with preventing war materials or contraband from reaching Germany whose sea doors to the outer world were via the North Sea, English Channel and Mediterranean.

Britain's first act of war in August 1914 was the blockading of all these seaways by the Royal Navy. The aim was to cast a ring of steel around Germany and keep tightening the ring until economic strangulation could be achieved. Despite all the terror inflicted by the U-boats throughout the war years, the British blockade held to the bitter end and was undoubtedly a factor in breaking the German will. The blockade very soon extended to cover every imaginable commodity, including food, from reaching Germany. It became known in Germany as the 'hunger blockade' and later the 'starvation blockade'. The German government was forced to take over grain shipments and control food distribution as rationing became necessary.

The blockade began to bite in earnest when, in November 1914, Britain declared the whole of the North Sea to be a military area, in breach of international law and the Paris Declaration. Britain maintained her blockade by laying extensive minefields in the English Channel and the North Sea, in support of Royal Navy patrols. Incoming freighters were now compelled to divert into designated English ports and submit to search and examination of their cargoes by the navy. Those found shipping contraband to Germany were subject to confiscation of ship and cargo. Those whose bona fides were in order were allowed to proceed by being escorted through known minefields by the Royal Navy. This caused great inconvenience and friction to neutral ships normally destined for Norway, the Baltic, Denmark and Holland. Long delays were endured in crowded ports while searches were carried out. The Royal Navy did not dare search freighters on the open seas as they would be exposed to submarine attack; neutral America was furious at the disruption to trade and loss of business by being cut off from their European trading partners. America even wondered whether Britain was trying to ruin its overseas trade in order to enhance her own.

The Rules of Blockade were codified at the Paris Declaration in 1856. Britain joined the other great powers of Europe as a signatory to that declaration. At the Paris Declaration it was generally agreed that the highways of the seas belonged to all nations of the world and all should have the right to sail them. The issue is more aptly referred to as the Freedom of the Seas. In broad terms, Britain should have imposed her blockade at the edge of German territorial waters only, known as the three-mile limit. Such action would be legal and in compliance with the Paris Declaration. The British Admiralty knew only too well that their warships would not stand a chance of surviving blockade patrols so close to mainland Germany. As well as being sitting ducks for U-boats, there were numerous other natural hazards such as shoaling reefs and tiny islands that were bound to impale their ships in time of fog or poor visibility.

The island of Heligoland, about forty miles off the German coast, was a veritable fortress of powerful long-range guns. The newly invented airship and aeroplane could drop bombs from the air. Britain, to justify its illegal long range blockade, was quick to parade all these excuses to an infuriated America. In retaliation for the hunger blockade, Germany imposed its own counter blockade by declaring all the waters around the British Isles to be a war zone from 4 February 1915. They further warned that ships entering the area would be liable to destruction without warning and that it would not always be possible to prevent attacks on neutral shipping. Von Tirpitz was optimistic that his new strategy would starve Britain into submission in a short time. Each country was now attempting to starve its opponent, one with a blockade of ships above the sea, and the other with a blockade of submarines beneath the ocean waves.

The early months of the war saw Germany with a total of twenty-eight operational U-boats. Of that number, an average of one-third could be found setting out on patrol, one-third returning back to base in Germany for replenishment of fuel and torpedoes, and the remainder undergoing repair and refit.

This small fleet was deployed to various locations around the British Isles with three designated for the South Western Approaches which covered the stretch of water from Fastnet extending up the southern Irish coast and the Irish Sea. This proved to be a very fruitful area for targets. The intended victims were usually steaming to, or from, America and out of such ports as Liverpool, Queenstown or Milfordhaven. The best killing areas proved to be around Fastnet, Galley Head, Kinsale, Queenstown and Waterford. U-boat commanders referred to this stretch of water as Torpedo Alley. Destruction was inflicted on Allied shipping by torpedo, mine or shells from the U-boat's gun.

An entirely different category of submarines known as the UC class, or minelayers, were also regular visitors to the same waters as they laid their deadly cargoes of mines around the entrances to harbours and on main shipping lanes. Once they had laid their mines they returned silently and unobserved to their base.

The early type UC-boats were minelayers only, and as such were not equipped with torpedoes or guns; instead they were fitted with six mine chutes which could accommodate twelve mines. These innovative craft proved to be another unwelcome surprise for the Admiralty. UC-boats deposited their mines which were attached to weighted sinkers and pre-coiled wire rope-moorings as they sank to the seabed. Having been submerged for some hours, a soluble plug would dissolve in the release mechanism of the mine, causing it to float to the surface. As the mine bobbed up and down on the waves it was still attached to the sinker weight by a light wire-rope tether. The tether maintained the floating mine at its designated location in a harbour or shipping lane, where it was hoped it would inflict maximum damage to passing ships. This delay caused by the soluble plugs in the sinker weight mechanisms was essential to give the minelayer ample time to get well clear of the deadly mine-field it had just laid. The release mechanisms were notoriously unreliable with the result that mines often exploded prematurely as they were released from their chutes, causing the untimely death of all hands on board. This tendency to 'self-destroy' earned the UC-boats the nickname Sisters of Sorrow.

Initially, submarines leaving Germany headed for Ireland via the Dover Straits. This shortcut route was soon closed off by the British use of mine barrages, wire nets and patrol boats; it meant that marauding

U-boats now had to take the northern route around Scotland and down the west coast of Ireland to reach the hunting ground, adding 1,400 miles to each round trip. The British refused to believe that U-boats were capable of such long journeys and were instead convinced that they were still somehow penetrating the Dover defences. This false notion actually led Churchill to sack Commander Hood for negligence in allowing mythical submarines to pass under his nose. Hood was demoted to Queenstown where he was entrusted with command of a motley and obsolete fleet of small patrol boats. He was later reinstated when the Admiralty realised that they had grossly underestimated the U-boats' radius of action. Unfortunately, promotion sounded the death knell for Hood who lost his life in the 1916 Battle of Jutland.

The U-boat campaign was also waged in the Mediterranean. In late 1915, Germany decided to copy the British tactic of misusing flags. As America had not yet entered the war, Germany was sensitive to the sinking of ships that might have Americans on board. The ruthless U-boat ace, Max Valentiner, skirted this problem by using false colours; he regularly flew the Austrian flag when committing his victims to the deep. However, it proved to be the last straw for the Austrians when Valentiner used their flag while sinking liners and hospital ships. The Austrian Emperor, Franz Josef, lost his patience and demanded that Germany desist from the practice; Berlin eventually complied and accordingly issued orders to its U-boat flotillas on the high seas. Confidence in the U-boat grew rapidly and 1917 saw 111 submarines in service. They had also increased their range with some even reaching America; others marauded in the Barents Sea as they scoured the Arctic trade routes; some patrolled off the Canary Islands and some went to fight in the Turkish campaign in Gallipoli. Allied shipping was now being lost much faster than it could be replaced and the Admiralty coldly calculated that they would be defeated by November 1917 if counter-measures could not be found to stem the carnage. Finally, after much heated debate, the Admiralty reluctantly agreed to the convoy system. This meant that, in future, merchant ships would assemble in large groups and all steam together while being escorted to their destinations by Royal Navy warships. The hidebound attitudes of the Admirals decreed that it was beneath the dignity of ships of the Royal Navy to escort these groups of old rag-tag rusty freighters; this duty belittled what the Navy stood for. Another countermeasure against the U-boats could be taken by using the newly invented depth charge. If U-boats were suspected of lurking in certain areas, the depth charges could be dropped in their vicinity. The sinking depth charge exploded by hydrostatic pressure and depth settings could be adjusted to maximise results. Finally, British Intelligence, which had blundered for three years at the hands of Admiral Oliver and others, was given a new lease on life when the old Admiral was replaced in 1917 by a new director named Geddes. This energetic young man eliminated various bureaucratic log-jams and streamlined the system, ensuring that intelligence regarding U-boats disposition was passed on promptly to navy ships at sea. At last the new countermeasures turned the tide of Allied shipping losses. The haemorrhage had been stemmed and Britain could see chinks of light and hope in the abyss of defeat.

5

The Codebreakers

IT IS NECESSARY TO ACQUAINT the reader with the Admiralty headquarters in Whitehall, London, and in particular an Intelligence department within that building known as Room 40. British Intelligence played a silent and sinister role in the sinking of the *Lusitania,* and the subsequent scapegoating of the unfortunate Captain Turner in order to deflect public attention from their own guilt and attempts to cover up their gross negligence.

At the outbreak of the First World War in 1914, the British Post Office and the Marconi company began to record wireless telegraphy (Morse) transmissions, apparently of German origin. The information they contained was disguised by codes and ciphers, and was obviously meaningless without the means by which they could be deciphered. It was felt that the mystery transmissions were in some way related to the war, therefore they were passed on to the Admiralty's Director of Intelligence in Whitehall. Britain had failed to set up a codebreaking organisation before the war and it had no experience or expertise in dealing with codes. This resulted in the incoming messages accumulating on the director's desk until they could find some means of dealing with them. However, Churchill, who was First Lord of the Admiralty in 1914, was soon to receive a priceless gift to help solve the dilemma.

On 25 August 1914, two German warships, the *Augsburg* and the *Magdeburg*, were on a mission of reconnaissance in the Gulf of Finland. The mission proved to be uncomfortably close for the Russians whose main naval base was in nearby Kronstadt. Early on 26 August, the two ships encountered dense fog causing the *Magdeburg* to run hard aground on an island off Russian Estonia. When the fog lifted, the *Magdeburg* plight was revealed to the Russians who responded with guns blazing from two of their warships which happened to be in the vicinity. In the confusion, the Russians managed to capture a vital set of code books from the *Magdeburg,* before her commander had time to destroy them along with other secret papers.

The Russians later instructed their naval attaché in London to offer the code books to Churchill if he would be kind enough to send a warship to North Russia. HMS *Theseus* departed for Russia in

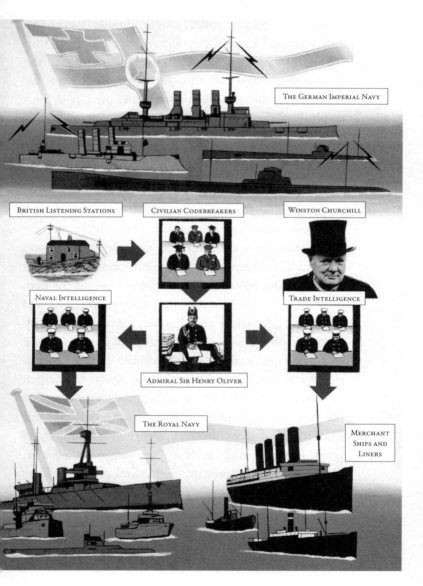

THE GERMAN IMPERIAL NAVY

BRITISH LISTENING STATIONS

CIVILIAN CODEBREAKERS

WINSTON CHURCHILL

NAVAL INTELLIGENCE

TRADE INTELLIGENCE

ADMIRAL SIR HENRY OLIVER

THE ROYAL NAVY

MERCHANT SHIPS AND LINERS

September 1914 to collect the invaluable documents and returned on 13 October to deliver them into Churchill's hands. Churchill fully appreciated the inestimable value of this Intelligence victory for Britain and the need to maintain the utmost secrecy to preserve their integrity. Only a tiny charmed circle within the Admiralty was aware of the existence of the *Magdeburg* codes, namely Admirals Wilson, Oliver, Fisher, Captain Hall and, of course, Churchill who drew up the charter for a new codebreaking or cryptographic division. Churchill drew up this charter in his own hand and headed it Exclusively Secret.

The task of setting up this new department was entrusted to Admiral Oliver who knew nothing of cryptography. However, Oliver wisely sought the help of a colleague, Sir Alfred Ewing, who was the Director of Naval Education and known for his interest in cryptography. It was soon realised that the expertise to tackle codebreaking was not available from within the Royal Navy and Ewing had to resort to civilian volunteers to help him set up his new cryptographic division. These civilians consisted mainly of dons from Oxford, professors from Cambridge, headmasters from Eton as well as from the naval colleges of Osborne and Dartmouth. Like Admiral Oliver, they knew nothing of codes and ciphers, but were very willing to learn in the interest of serving king and country. Their discretion could be relied upon in the execution of their most secret work. Some were brilliant mathematicians while others were German linguists. The original group of less than ten people was installed on the first floor of the old Admiralty building in London occupying room number forty. As an official name had not yet been considered for this new group of codebreakers, they were merely referred to as Room 40 OB. The name stuck and remained unchanged throughout the First World War.

The Admiralty in those early days was over-centralised, inefficient and generally aloof from their naval staff. More gold braid was taken to mean more intelligence, orders had to be obeyed without question and initiative from subordinates was stifled.

Admirals were snobbish and overbearing in their attitudes. Captains commanded their ships but only the Admiralty was capable of deciding the higher conduct of war. Admiral Oliver, the father of Room 40, had all these attributes and more; he was contemptuous of the work of others; he despised his codebreakers because they were civilians; their opinions were left unsolicited, and they were never consulted about their work. As civilians, most of the codebreakers had no knowledge of naval parlance and were mocked for their ignorance of these matters. One of the decoding staff once submitted a decode which stated that 'a ship ran' to a certain destination. He was ridiculed by the First Sea Lord, Jacky Fisher, and told that ships do not 'run' but rather 'proceed'.

The excessive secrecy of the Churchill charter required the codebreakers to communicate their knowledge only to Admiral Oliver. They were not permitted to erect a chart on the wall where they could easily plot the positions of the German fleet and their submarines. They were not allowed to pass on the fruits of their work to the Naval Intelligence Division (NID) which, in turn, was responsible for passing on information to the Royal Navy, nor were they allowed to pass on information to the Trade Division which was responsible for the safety of British merchant ships at sea. The headmasters and other civilian staff of Room 40 took some weeks to figure out how the various keys and ciphers of the *Magdeburg* documents could be applied to the coded messages on their desks. However, having achieved their first success they became very adept, and eventually managed to decipher a code in a record-breaking time of twenty minutes.

This tiny band of men performed brilliantly throughout the war and were said to be the only group of people who really knew what the German Navy was up to, at any given moment. Some deciphered messages only contained useless trivia such as information about the contents of a ship's diesel tanks or its coal reserves. However, even the most insignificant messages could play a vital role in identifying that ship's position.

The British had set up a number of DF (Direction Finding) stations along the coast of Britain and

Ireland. By this means, a German warship or submarine would betray its position by merely using its radio. German wireless messages were liable to arrive at any hour of the day or night. The tiny band of codebreakers were always willing to tackle them immediately, though often in a jaded state from overwork and lack of sleep. Once the messages were converted to plain language, they were passed on to the operations division for scrutiny by Admiral Oliver. In spite of the fact that the septuagenarian Oliver was a workaholic, there was no way he could cope with the huge workload single-handedly. Oliver examined each decode on arrival at his desk and then re-drafted his own interpretation of the contents before passing on the message to the naval or trade divisions. He believed that only he could interpret the true meaning of the decodes. In effect, he watered down the precise meaning of the decodes and dissipated their valuable contents. For example, on one occasion Oliver learned from a decode that a U-boat was due to appear on a certain day outside Barrow-in-Furness. He re-drafted the message to read that the said U-boat was to appear to the west of England. On some occasions messages were tampered with by Admiral Oliver to such a degree that they appeared to mean the opposite of the original version by the time they reached the hand of the Commander-in-Chief of the Royal Navy, Sir John Jellicoe. Oliver was so obsessed with secrecy that he failed to realise that a secret is not worth keeping unless you can make some use of it. Another disastrous practice of Oliver's was to pass on vital information twelve to twenty hours after he had received it from the Room 40 team. Old intelligence is generally useless intelligence. The delay was attributable to Admiral Oliver's intransigence in not delegating a portion of his staggering workload to others.

In March 1915, Fisher wrote in a memo to Churchill, *'Oliver so overburdens himself that he is twenty-four hours behind with his basket of papers.'* Jellicoe, commander of the Grand Fleet in Scapa Flow, was unaware of the existence of Room 40 and regularly complained to the Admiralty about their practice of sitting too long on vital information. He sometimes consigned Oliver's notes to the waste paper basket, as he deemed them to be inaccurate and unreliable.

Admiral Oliver ran Room 40 as his own personal cryptographic department. He would delegate only the most menial task as he felt that nobody could do anything except himself. On rare occasions when he was ill or away from his desk, his department ground to a halt until his return. He resisted any attempts to communicate with his civilian staff and mistakes were inevitable as a result.

Churchill kept in close touch with the day-to-day happenings by authorising Commander Hall to sift through the multiplicity of messages and give him a daily summary of events as they unfolded. Admiral Oliver gave little consideration to the safety of merchant ships – only such merchant ships as carried munitions or other war-related cargoes warranted much attention. This category included the passenger liners as they were liable to be recalled at any time for wartime duties.

When Admiral Oliver learned from a decode that an important merchant ship might be in danger, he would draft a note in his own hand to suggest counter-measures to be taken by that ship to ensure its safety. The Trade Division, controlled by Captain Webb, passed these messages on to ships in danger. Counter-measures, in the case of merchant ships, usually meant diverting a ship in danger to the nearest port to await an escort of destroyers to accompany it through the danger zone. Alternatively, a ship in port might be instructed not to leave that port until the sea could be cleared of mines and submarines. However, most merchant ships could not be warned, as they did not have wireless on board to receive such instructions. Wireless was very much in its infancy during the First World War period.

Unfortunately, the brilliant work of the decoders suffered from a faulty system imposed from above. Room 40 had a very precise knowledge of the disposition of the German Navy and its submarines; however, they had no idea of the existence of the Naval Intelligence Division, let alone the disposition of the Royal Navy's ships at sea. The navy was equally unaware of the existence of Room 40 or the disposition of the

German Navy's ships. The same farce extended to the Trade Division, which had some knowledge of the disposition of the merchant ships but none at all in relation to the German, or Royal Navy's dispositions.

The excessive secrecy of Churchill's charter meant that each of these vital departments worked in isolation from their counterparts. Had the combined knowledge of the three departments been put on a chart, the danger to shipping would become immediately obvious and a lot of information would have been gleaned. Faulty positioning of Royal Navy ships could have been corrected and they could have been diverted to locations where they might be better employed in safeguarding convoys or lone merchant ships. Better countermeasures could be taken in the light of more accurate knowledge. If only Admiral Oliver had refrained from his tendency to dilute decodes, he would have been able to send more accurate information to Allied shipping. If only messages were sent on time and not twelve to twenty hours too late when they were of little use. Had all these factors been considered and implemented, there is no doubt that it would have saved the lives of thousands of civilians and servicemen, not to mention hundreds of thousands of tons of Allied shipping.

In spite of its inefficient management from 1914 to 1917, Room 40 had been advantageous in many ways. It had disclosed the routes taken by German warships and submarines; it had reduced the number of ships required to be kept at sea on patrol duty; and it gave advance warning of German naval intentions, thus enabling the Royal Navy to go into a state of high alert each time the Germans planned a move with their fleet. Room 40 intercepted and decoded many messages relating to German assistance to the planned Easter Rebellion in Ireland in 1916.

On 9 April of that year, the German gun-running ship *Aud* set out on a mission to deliver arms to Ireland for a planned uprising. The ship carried on board 20,000 captured Russian rifles, 10 machine guns, and 1 million rounds of ammunition as well as explosives. The *Aud* reached Tralee Bay in the southwest of Ireland but was intercepted by a British warship and escorted to Queenstown. However, the gunrunner was scuttled by its crew before reaching its destination and sank at the mouth of Cork Harbour with its cargo of weapons. Roger Casement, who organised the shipment, was quickly arrested, convicted of treason, and condemned to be hanged. Casement was a former servant of the British Crown, from whom he had accepted a knighthood.

However, there was much sympathy for Casement in the United States and parts of England. Pressure was put on the British government by America to commute the death sentence by a vigorous Save Casement campaign. To counteract this pressure, Captain Reggie Hall, who was Director of Naval Intelligence, in conjunction with the head of

Scotland Yard, Sir Basil Thomson, leaked portions of the notorious Black Diaries to the public. The diaries contained accounts of Casement's supposed homosexual activities. Support for Casement ended abruptly at the shock revelations and he was hanged in Pentonville Prison on 3 August 1916. Many experts at the time claimed the diaries to be forgeries and the controversy still rages today over the issue. Modern textual analysis would seem to lend credence to the forgery theory. Reggie Hall had abundant evidence of Casement's activities in plotting with the Germans; this evidence was contained in the Berlin Intercepts which dealt with Casement's attempts to organise insurrection by Irish revolutionaries in America. However, Hall could not use this information at Casement's trial for fear of betraying the existence of Room 40 to the Germans.

Before we leave Captain Reggie Hall, some further comment on his background is warranted since he rose from the position of captain to admiral as a result of his brilliant achievements as Director of Naval Intelligence. Hall was born into a Royal Navy family in 1870. He joined that navy at the age of fourteen and specialised in gunnery. He was promoted to captain in 1905. During his sea years he had a natural aptitude for covert intelligence and cloak-and-dagger work. He was decommissioned from the navy on grounds of ill health and became Director of Naval Intelligence at the Admiralty in October 1914. He was fascinated by the world of spies, double agents, deception, bribery, disinformation, de-stabilisation, skulduggery and dirty tricks in general. Hall was not familiar with the finer points of code breaking but he certainly knew how to make best use of the results.

Hall became the 'Man of Room 40' by single-handedly leaking the contents of the Zimmerman telegram thus persuading the reluctant American President Wilson to declare war on Germany in April 1917.

As Britain was brought to the brink of defeat in the early months of 1917, Lloyd George, the Prime Minister, sensed that something was radically wrong with the methods of Room 40 and took steps to re-organise and de-centralise the whole structure of the Admiralty which controlled it.

In May 1917, Sir Eric Geddes was appointed to take over the administration and control of the whole department. Geddes was an extremely able forty-one-year-old director of North Eastern Railways and something of an efficiency expert and businessman supreme. When he took over the running of the Admiralty, he was appalled at the inefficiency he found there. To help him blend in with his reluctant colleagues he was given the honorary title of Vice Admiral with a uniform to match; his new position saw the age-old battle of the 'young bull' versus the 'old' being played out in the corridors of the Admiralty in London.

Admiral Oliver was full of contempt for Geddes and his efforts to introduce modern business methods and streamlining to the Admiralty. Geddes re-organised the Admiralty against opposition and inertia shown to him by entrenched admirals with unbending attitudes. The long delays in passing on information were eliminated; a special submarine tracking room was set up; a wall chart was erected and positions of ships and submarines were plotted. The decoders, Naval Intelligence and trade divisions worked in cooperation instead of in isolation. Initiative was now encouraged and not stifled, even from officers of low rank. The problem of understaffing in the codebreaking section was addressed, and the group expanded to include new civilian volunteers from all walks of life. Some were clergymen, bankers, stockbrokers, businessmen. Geddes succeeded in streamlining Room 40 and producing an organisation of great finesse. There is no doubt that Room 40 was instrumental in defeating the U-boats.

Room 40 robbed the Germans of the advantage of surprise and was a contributory factor in the final victory of the British, French, Italian, Belgian and American armies in 1918. Had the Royal Navy lost control of the sea routes of the world, the prosecution of the war could have been markedly different. The British and American armies could never have reached the field of battle, nor could the European armies of the entente have held out without their support.

Churchill once drew a comparison between the war at sea and the daily routine of Room 40. When the navy did battle, the atmosphere was filled with the deafening thunder of big guns and bursting shells, accompanied by the acrid smell of cordite and skies aflame. By comparison, the loudest noise to be heard in Room 40 was the ticking of the clock. Quiet men with quick steps would enter and depart, having left pencilled slips of paper on desks for deciphering. The codebreakers would scribble lines and calculations, sometimes in silence and other times in a subdued murmur. Those on night watch often strove to fight off the desperate desire to sleep, but found that the desire vanished on the arrival of a fresh message to be decoded. Although little-known or appreciated by the general public, their silent work was often as valuable in effect as that of the thunderous guns in the faraway mists of the North Sea.

The torch that was Room 40 died to a glowing ember shortly after the war ended in November 1918. However, it was the forerunner of the immensely successful codebreaking division, Bletchley Park.

6

A Sinister Silence

UP TO THE MONTH of April 1915, the U-boat campaign was directed towards a war against commerce, in support of Germany's stated objective of declaring the waters around the British Isles to be a war zone from 4 February 1915. Germany had further warned that any ships entering this area would be subject to destruction and it would not always be possible to warn neutral ships due to Britain's misuse of flags. In stalking merchant ships U-boats avoided British patrols and warships whenever possible by merely diving beneath the waves where they could not be detected. As far as the south coast of Ireland was concerned, the blockading schedule usually meant one U-boat on patrol, one returning to base for repairs and replenishment of its torpedoes and fuel, and one setting out to relieve its patrolling partner. Patrols usually lasted for four days and commanders tended to make the return journey when their fuel levels dictated that they do so.

However, in April 1915, the Imperial German Navy saw reason to suspend the U-boat blockade schedule in light of new information received. Captain Hall, of Room 40 fame, had leaked misinformation to Germany, via his Intelligence department, that there would be heavy sailings of transports from west and south coast ports in Britain. To this day, nobody has offered an explanation for Hall's action. Germany received Hall's misinformation on 24 April 1915 and took the matter very seriously indeed. In the months leading up to April 1915, Germany had been expecting a major naval offensive against its coast and even anticipated an invasion would occur in Schleswig-Holstein supported by troop landings. In response to this imaginary threat, German U-boat command instructed its submarines to take immediate steps to seek out and attack these transports. U-boats large and small were diverted from other theatres of operation to maraud off British ports and disrupt the much-feared troop movements out of these ports. The U-30 was already underway on 25 April when she received new instructions by German radio. As well as being given changed orders she was advised of the anticipated large troop movements from British ports. U-30 was re-routed to take up station outside Dartmouth; she was also ordered to attack transports, merchant ships and warships. She was to remain on station for as long as supplies lasted. She was also informed of the future orders and instructions to U-20 to proceed to the Irish Sea and Bristol Channel. All this information was intercepted by Room 40 and the threat to shipping became immediately obvious. On 7 May, the U-20 would torpedo the *Lusitania* off Kinsale. Destiny had allowed Admiral Oliver twelve days in which to decide what measures could be taken to safeguard one of Britain's greatest liners.

On 30 April, Room 40 intercepted another signal from German radio which confirmed that the *Lusitania's* nemesis, the U-20, had been sighted and was on its way. The U-20 was commanded by Walter Schwieger as it set out around northern Scotland at the start of its patrol. Schwieger avoided enemy warships off Peterhead as he sailed through the Fair Isle channel on 2 May. That night, he sighted a large Danish steamer but was not in suitable position to attack. The next day Schwieger sighted a steamer of 2,000 tons and swung into battle stations to attack; fortunately for the steamer, Schwieger's torpedo jammed in its tube and the attempt was a failure. As he continued his journey down the west coasts of Scotland and Ireland, he noted in his diary that the weather was generally bad. On the evening of 4 May, Schwieger attacked the neutral Swedish steamer *Hibernia* but missed his target. By 5 May, he was off the Old Head of Kinsale and proceeding eastwards; here he sighted a small sailing ship named the *Earl of Lathom* which he deemed safe to attack on the surface. Schwieger first allowed the five crew members time to launch their lifeboat and row a safe distance away, before his men placed bombs on board and sank the sailing ship. U-boats generally sunk small ships by bomb or gunfire from their deck gun as they could not justify wasting an expensive torpedo on a ship of minor significance. Schwieger proceeded eastwards on his intended mission and encountered another ship, the *Cayo Romano,* four hours later in the vicinity of Daunt Rock outside Cork Harbour. He attempted, without success, to torpedo this ship which ran for the safety of Queenstown Harbour. Late that evening both incidents had been reported by the survivors to Queenstown who, in turn, informed the Admiralty in London before 10 p.m., on the same day. This was the first inkling Queenstown had of the presence of a submarine outside its harbour; it was also positive proof that a submarine existed. The Admiralty in London were already aware of the U-20 incursion and its intended patrol from earlier Room 40 intercepts. Inexplicably, the Admiralty had not seen fit to pass on this vital intelligence to Queenstown, even though it was in its possession for the previous ten days. Other areas under threat from the U-20 were Milfordhaven and Liverpool, which were also deprived of the Admiralty's important information.

In response to the appearance of a submarine outside its doorstep, Queenstown broadcast a plain language message to all ships at 10.30 p.m. warning that a U-boat was active off the southern Irish coast. This message was surprisingly vague when compared to the precise knowledge Admiral Coke of Queenstown had gleaned from the survivors of the *Earl of Lathom* and the near-miss account from the crew of the *Cayo Romano*. No special warning was sent to the oncoming *Lusitania* known to be converging on the same track as the U-20. At this stage the *Lusitania* was still several hundred miles west of the Fastnet and steaming at twenty-one knots.

Walter Schwieger proceeded eastwards in the deteriorating visibility and surfaced early in the morning of 6 May near Coningbeg Lightship, off the Waterford coast. Here he encountered the British steamship *Candidate,* a vessel of 3,826 tons. The ship attempted to escape but the U-20 gave chase while firing all the time with its single deck gun. The *Candidate* took numerous hits from U-20's gun and was forced to stop eventually when her fire gang refused to man the boiler room any longer. John Light had reason to believe, from his researches, that the striking crew of the boiler room may have been courtmartialled and shot for deserting their post. In any case, the crew of the *Candidate* were allowed time to abandon ship before Schwieger launched a torpedo which exploded but failed to sink the ship. Schwieger was forced to open fire once again with his deck gun to assist in the sinking of his victim. A few hours later, around midday, another steamer emerged out of the fog; it was the 15,000 ton White Star liner *Arabic*. Schwieger again attempted to torpedo this passenger liner but was prevented from doing so when fog descended and blinded his view. Unfortunately the reprieve was brief; the *Arabic* fell victim to a torpedo of the U-24 only three months later and sank off the Old Head of Kinsale, not many miles from the final resting place of the *Lusitania*. Late in the evening of 6 May, Schwieger's luck returned when he let off a torpedo, without warning, at another British freighter, the 3,854 ton *Centurion*. His victim stubbornly refused to sink and he was obliged to fire a second torpedo to complete the job; survivors of both these ships were rescued and brought ashore at Milfordhaven. The authorities still made no serious attempt to warn the *Lusitania* as she headed straight into the path of the U-20. Only general instructions were broadcast nightly to all shipping covering such diverse locations as Dover, Folkestone and St George's Channel. By 8.55 a.m. on 7 May, both the Admiralty in London and Queenstown were fully aware of the loss of the Waterford steamers. However, the Admiralty were very concerned about the threat posed by U-20 from the moment they first learned from Room 40 of her intended patrol on 25 April and again on 30 April.

A British battleship, the HMS *Orion*, had completed a refit at Devonport and was required urgently back with the Grand Fleet in Scapa Flow. On 2 May, Oliver drafted a note in his own hand suggesting that the *Orion* be held in port in view of the potential danger from U-20; she eventually sailed on 4 May with an escort of four destroyers. She was further given orders about course and advised to keep 100 miles off the southern Irish coast.

Similarly the cruiser HMS *Gloucester* was returning from Gibraltar and was given specific instructions about course change and speed to keep it well clear of Schwieger's submarine. Yet another battleship, the HMS *Jupiter,* was returning from duty in north Russia for repairs to her ice-damaged hull. These were to be carried out at Barrow-in-Furness. The *Jupiter* was given a course change and diverted down to Barrow via the northern channel past Larne; as a further safety measure, she was also given an escort of destroyers. In these three examples, Oliver's actions and countermeasures to safeguard his ships are very commendable; they also offer ample proof that the Admiralty clearly recognised the danger posed to shipping by the presence of a patrolling submarine.

On the evening of 6 May, Schwieger took a decision not to proceed to Liverpool. In his diary he gives fog and bad weather generally as his reasons. Without visibility, Schwieger could not stalk his prey in the busy waters outside the Mersey; strong enemy patrols and destroyers could be expected and he would be in grave danger of being run down or rammed on sight; he recorded in his log: *'Surface action against transports leaving Liverpool impossible except in clear weather and at night, as escorting destroyers cannot be sighted in time.'* Dwindling fuel levels also decided Schwieger's return; he had hoped to encounter, and attack, more steamers off Bristol on his return as it was less heavily defended than Liverpool. Shortly after 11 a.m. on 7 May, Schwieger was making his return journey underwater when he heard a ship pass over him at high speed. When the thudding of her engines had faded, he came to periscope depth and noted the battle cruiser, HMS *Juno,* heading for Queenstown. Earlier, at 7.45 a.m., *Juno* had received a specific warning from the Admiralty concerning the U-boat danger off Queenstown. On that morning, 7 May, public hysteria broke out on the streets of Liverpool following the loss of the two steamers off Waterford.

The chairman of Cunard, Sir Alfred Booth, was obliged to make haste to the senior naval officer and request that he warn the oncoming *Lusitania* about what was now a very grave situation. This prompted a vague response from the authorities when another message to 'all ships' was transmitted at 11.15 a.m. warning that: '... *U-boats were active in the southern part of the Irish channel, last heard of twenty miles south of Coningbeg Lightship* ...' This vague information was already twenty hours old and of questionable value so long after the event.

At 2.20 p.m. on 7 May, Schwieger sighted a four-funnel ship which he identified as a large liner. U-20 dived within minutes and set a new course to intercept the oncoming ship. At 3.10 p.m. Schwieger was within 700 yards of the *Lusitania* when he launched a single torpedo at her starboard bow; the torpedo exploded just under her bridge and approximately half a minute later was followed by a huge internal explosion in the forward part of the ship and a violent emission of smoke far above the foremost funnel. Schwieger noted in his log that an exceptionally heavy detonation had taken place with a great explosive cloud reaching far across the first funnel. Schwieger attributed the explosion to 'boilers, powder or coal'. Captain Turner of the *Lusitania* also noticed the strong detonation, which he believed was due to ruptured steam lines or exploding boilers. In 1966 the late John de Courcy Ireland interviewed Lieutenant Raymond Wiesbach, the man who launched the torpedo against the oncoming *Lusitania* on that fateful day off the Old Head of Kinsale. Wiesbach wrote a full account of his experiences; his statement also noted an exceptionally heavy detonation. He did not get an opportunity to look in the periscope as Schwieger led the attack throughout. Subsequent to the explosion Schwieger noted that the superstructure above the bridge was torn away and fire had broken out. The ship took a heavy list immediately with the bow dipping beneath the sea; he now noted the name *Lusitania* in large brass letters and that her funnels were painted black; he also concluded that the ship would soon sink and he decided to dive to twenty-four metres, thus departing the scene. Within the next eighteen minutes, the *Lusitania* had sunk beneath the waves to her perpetual resting place twelve miles off the Old Head of Kinsale; civilian loss of life totalled 1,198 passengers and crew including 94 children and 140 neutral American citizens. Within the next few hours, a relatively obscure U-boat commander, Walter Schwieger, would become the most hated man on earth as a flame of indignation swept around the whole world.

Before we leave the subject of the Admiralty's reckless disregard for the *Lusitania*'s safety, it is useful to examine other incidents where lesser merchant ships received warnings and protection from those same authorities in similar circumstances. When submarine danger threatened, the Admiralty's prime concern was the safety of the Grand Fleet (Royal Navy). The protection or warning of merchants ships was of secondary importance and applied only to ships with important government cargoes or ships that might be of value to the war effort; liners such as the *Lusitania* qualified for the latter category as they proved to be invaluable for transporting large numbers of troops or serving as hospital ships. Toward the end of January 1915, the Admiralty learned from an intercept that the U-21 was setting out on a mission via the English Channel to patrol the area around Barrow-in-Furness on the northwest coast of England.

Oliver took energetic steps to warn a large number of authorities including Queenstown, Liverpool, Pembroke, Belfast, Larne, Mull of Kintyre, Tor Head and the Grand Fleet. The intentions of U-21 to maraud outside Barrow were clearly revealed to the above authorities. Two Cunard liners, the *Transylvania* and the *Ausonia,* were diverted to Queenstown to await destroyer escort; the passengers of both ships were held in port for several days and some, who were neutral Americans, were furious to discover that both liners carried large guns for the navy. The *Transylvania* was captained by Turner and had two 15-inch guns lashed to its decks by ring bolts; the guns were 53 feet long and 5 feet across the breech. Each weighed 75 tons and were manufactured by Bethlehem Steel Corporation, the chief American armourers to World War One. Behind the two guns were a single gun turret and various boxes of parts associated with the guns. The incident begs the question of Oliver's concern: was it because of the large deck guns needed for the war, or the threat to passenger lives, that he took such commendable action? The discovery of this unusual cargo revealed Cunard's policy of mixing civilians with contraband of war on their liners.

As a further measure to curb the U-21 incursion to the Irish sea, a fleet of destroyers was ordered to sweep down from the Grand Fleet in the north and attempt to intercept and sink the raider. In support of this action yet another fleet of destroyers from the Harwich force was ordered to sweep up from the south in pursuit of the marauder. However, the daring U-21 sank three ships and escaped back to Germany intact. Meanwhile its comrade, U-20, had been operating in the English Channel where it sank three ships and torpedoed and missed a hospital ship, the *Asturias*. It was the January activities of these two submarines that spawned the idea of Q Ships, flag misuse and the secret ram order.

Another example of Admiralty concern can be seen when one looks at events that occurred in February 1915. On 11 February, Admiralty Intelligence learned that the submarine U-30 was setting out on a mission to the west. This potential threat to the Irish Sea caused the Admiralty to strengthen patrols and increase destroyer presence in hopes of intercepting the U-30. By 20 February, the submarine had reached the Irish Sea and sunk two ships; as a result two steamers, the *Armenian* and the *Hydaspes,* were diverted to Queenstown to await a destroyer escort to ensure safe completion of their voyage from America to Liverpool. Both ships had cargoes of mules for the Army; during their detention and wait for escorting warships, several horses died on board the ships. The *Armenian* was not so lucky four months later; she was en route from America to Liverpool when she was attacked and sunk by the U-38 off Cornwall. Twenty-nine men and 1,414 mules went down with the ship.

On 3 March 1915, Room 40 were again alarmed by an intercept from German radio in Neumunster to her submarines advising that the *Lusitania,* on her return voyage, was due at Liverpool on 4 or 5 March. At the request of the Cunard company the Trade Division of the Admiralty transmitted specific instructions to the *Lusitania* about its course and speed. Further concern was felt for her safety by Admiral Oliver when he ordered two destroyers out to meet the *Lusitania* and escort her back to port in spite of the fact that there was a grave shortage of destroyers at that particular moment. Oliver further ordered the Q ship, HMS *Lyons,* to patrol Liverpool Bay. The crises had barely passed when German radio again broadcast fresh information to their submarines; this time they advised that the *Lusitania* was due to depart from Liverpool bound for New York on 10 March. These various German broadcasts would seem to indicate that the *Lusitania* was firmly on the target list of the submarines. Oliver again showed concern for the safety of the *Lusitania* when he ordered that she be held in port until 20 March, when he could be sure that the area was clear of submarines; these various actions by Oliver are in striking contrast to his inactivity in relation to the final voyage of the *Lusitania*. Numerous questions were raised at the time and some remain unanswered today, almost a hundred years after the disaster. Could Oliver have sent out an escort of warships to shepherd the *Lusitania* safely into Liverpool and thus avert her date with destiny? The answer is a resounding 'yes', as four warships were available lying at anchor in Milfordhaven; these were HMS *Legion*, *Lucifer*, *Linnet* and *Laverock*. These four warships had been engaged in moving newly raised Irish regiments from Dublin to Liverpool; the movements took place over several nights in April; the final destination of the Irish regiments was the Dardanelles. After they had completed their work, they returned to Milfordhaven on 5 May to await orders. Also available were the Q ships *Baralong* and *Lyons*. No request for escort was made to this fleet of ships; why were these ships not sent out to hunt the U-20 when it revealed its presence by sinking the *Earl of Lathom*, the *Candidate* and the *Centurion*?

Why were no steps taken to protect the lives of over 2,000 innocent civilians on the *Lusitania* when such concern was shown only two months earlier to protect lesser ships transporting mules? Why were active measures taken on two occasions in March to protect the *Lusitania* because of a German radio broadcast? In previous submarine scares, various naval authorities were alerted to the danger; by stark contrast, the Queenstown naval authorities were not warned about the grave danger posed to the *Lusitania* by a submarine known to be converging on its path. Was Captain Hall's misinformation about troopship movements intended to entice further U-boats to the area west of England and create circumstances that might cause the loss of the *Lusitania*?

Why, in contrast to such specific information given to the likes of the *Orion*, *Gloucester*, *Jupiter* and *Juno*, should Captain Turner require less warning than these ships? His position was little different but, as history tells us, much more perilous.

At 7 a.m. on 7 May, the *Lusitania* was still about a hundred miles west of the Fastnet. Why was it not diverted around the north of Ireland and down past Larne on a similar course change as the *Jupiter*'s? Why was the *Lusitania* not diverted to Queenstown as in the cases of the *Ausonia*, *Transylvania*, *Hydaspes* and *Armenian*?

Even Schwieger had some questions to ask: U-boat attacks usually drew a rapid and much-feared response from Royal Navy ships appearing over the horizon to retaliate. Merchant ships at sea tended to run for cover and head for the nearest port until the danger had passed; those merchants not in favourable position to run for port were routinely given course changes by the Admiralty to divert them away from a submarine's track. On 7 May, Schwieger wrote in his log: *'It is remarkable that today there should be so much traffic despite the fact that two large steamers were sunk south of St George's Channel yesterday. It is inexplicable that the* Lusitania *was not routed via the North Channel.'*

The pieces of this difficult jigsaw puzzle would fit well together if we had proof that there was a grand plan by Churchill, Hall, Wilson, Oliver and Fisher to expose the *Lusitania* to the U-20 with a view to its subsequent destruction by torpedo. In a Machiavellian context, the loss of 1,198 civilian lives would be regrettable but would pale into insignificance when compared to the daily slaughter in the trenches of Europe. After all, in one single day in the Somme, 20,000 men lost their lives. If the *Lusitania* was sunk by submarine, American lives would surely be lost and neutral America would be enraged; before the loss of the *Lusitania*, a 5,800 ton steamship, named the *Falaba*, was torpedoed and sunk in the Irish channel with a loss of 104 lives including one American.

President Wilson interpreted the loss of the American life as a direct provocation of the United States. There was uproar in the American press and much resentment toward Germany. On 1 May, a ship named the *Gulflight* was torpedoed off the Scilly Isles; three American lives were lost, sparking off another diplomatic crisis. A submarine encounter with the *Lusitania* might be the trigger needed to persuade America to enter the war on the side of the Allies. The safety of Britain was at stake and defeat would be unthinkable; Britain would lose her Colonies and Empire and perhaps be reduced to starvation and bankruptcy; a powerful country like America, with its vast resources, could help the Allies sweep to victory; a victorious Britain would be in a position to confiscate any of Germany's crack liners to replace the sacrificed *Lusitania*. She subsequently did so by taking the *Imperator* and re-naming it the *Berengaria*. While there is no cast-iron proof of a conspiracy, there is abundant circumstantial evidence.

However, the conspiracy theory is diluted when one considers the contradictions against such a possibility. Britain was suffering a munitions crisis in 1915 and desperately needed shells for her army in France; the *Lusitania* shipped 5,000 of the much-needed shells on its final voyage. This was not an inconsiderable amount of shells when one realises that they occupied two cars of a freight train when transported to Pier 54 in New York for loading aboard the *Lusitania*; the consignment weighed over 50 tons. Also shipped on board were 4.2 million Remington cartridges consigned to army order. In addition, 18 cases of percussion fuses were included as well as 1,200 cubic feet of aluminium fine powder consigned to the explosives manufacturing division of the arsenal at Woolwich. In addition, almost 200 manifested sundry items on the *Lusitania*'s cargo were destined for the army or navy, though they were not of an explosive nature. It would seem highly illogical that the authorities would cram a ship's hatches full of such urgently-needed contraband of war if a plan was in place to deposit them at the bottom of the Atlantic a few days later. It should also be noted that Schwieger did not set out on his patrol with the express purpose of sinking the *Lusitania*; if he had received specific orders to do so he would not have betrayed his presence by sinking the *Earl of Lathom* or the two steamers off Waterford. His encounter was one of chance; if fog had not disrupted his plan, it seems likely that he would have directed all his energy and torpedoes to the Liverpool area. Ironically, the *Lusitania* was destined for that port and might still have come to grief nearer her destination.

7

The Town of the Dead

A SUNNY, carefree afternoon of 7 May 1915 found an unsuspecting *Lusitania* steaming approximately twelve miles southwest of the Old Head of Kinsale lighthouse. Passengers on deck enjoyed a light breeze as they viewed the emerald shores of Ireland. Suddenly, a disturbance was noticed on the mirror-calm sea off the starboard bow. This was followed by a thin streak of white foam as a single torpedo sped toward the *Lusitania* and exploded under its bridge. Like a stealthy assassin, Walter Schwieger had stalked the great ship and now struck without warning. His death-dealing torpedo ploughed into the side of his unwary victim. The first reaction aboard to the exploding torpedo was blank astonishment, followed by fear and an overwhelming sense of catastrophe. In the next eighteen minutes, Schwieger's action was to bring death, woe and desolation to the passengers and crew who numbered almost 2,000.

The Town of the Dead

The first explosion was quickly followed by a second, this time in the forward part of the ship. Splinters and wreckage rained down on those below. The ship began to list to starboard as the bow dipped into the sea. The work of extricating people from the debris was in progress when the call came for women and children to board the lifeboats. Captain Turner, frantically attempting to head the doomed *Lusitania* north towards land, soon found his crippled liner was out of control and would not respond to his efforts. Neither was he able to stop the engines to halt the ship and permit the lifeboats to be launched safely; he later attributed this to ruptured steamlines. Quickly following the explosions came a power cut, plunging the ship into darkness and bringing swarms of panic-stricken passengers out on deck. Throughout those eighteen minutes, as the mortally wounded ship sank under him, Turner stood calmly on the bridge giving instructions to his crew.

There were tearful scenes of parting as the lifeboats were lowered and women and children clambered on board. Husbands and fathers stood grim-faced and helpless, as many suspected the worst. The uncontrollable ship added to the terror by causing many lifeboats to capsize as they touched the ocean. Some of the occupants were tossed into the sea and had no chance of escape, as they had been torn or stunned by the explosion of the torpedo, scalded by escaping steam, or cut and maimed by flying debris. Shock also robbed some people of life, and of the hundreds rescued from the waters, many died of their injuries on the journey to shore in rescue boats. Saloon passengers had been at luncheon when the torpedo struck, and were shocked to come out on acutely listing decks, strewn with coal thrown up from the bunkers. It was still believed by some that the ship would remain afloat, so they stood back to allow others to avail themselves of the life-saving facilities that remained. Some, on the other hand, were hysterical, especially mothers with children. Captain Turner and his officers tried in vain to pacify them, while directing the launching of the lifeboats. This proved to be a fiasco. In many cases boats were undermanned before being launched, or manned by inexperienced personnel who could not keep them level as they were lowered to the sea. Lowering ropes were allowed to tangle and slip, or in some cases were abandoned, causing passengers to tumble into the sea as the lifeboats dangled vertically from the ends of their davits. Equipment was rusty and jammed, especially hinges and shackles. Collapsible rafts leaked badly and tended to swamp and capsize in the water.

In the mêlée, stewards and stewardesses hurriedly went among the passengers, handing out lifebelts and lifejackets. Their concern and attention to passengers safety was exemplary. The behaviour of some of the stokers, by comparison, was said to be too terrible for words as they rushed to board the boats with total disregard for others. One passenger stated that, if the crew got their just desserts, the stewards would be praised to heaven and the stokers damned to hell. As the liner settled deeper in the water, the efforts of crew and passengers became more frantic. Panic and tumult were everywhere as excited men and terrified women ran shouting around the decks. Lost children cried shrilly as officers and seamen rushed among the frantic passengers, shouting orders. Women clung desperately to their husbands while others knelt and prayed. The screams of the frightened men and women in the water added to the terror of those still on board. The list became so severe that passengers could no longer retain their footing and began to slide down the decks to meet the oncoming sea. Lifeboats launched on the high side of the ship had their planks ripped off as they bumped down the ship's side, which was cobbled with protruding rivet heads; boats already launched had to pull away as hard as they could to avoid being drawn under by the suction of the sinking ship. The rail on the upper deck was soon level with the sea as the end drew ever nearer.

The sun was still shining and the sea was dotted with hundreds of white faces, waterlogged boats, and bobbing heads of men who were still swimming. At first, people and debris in the water formed a tightly packed island which was later dispersed and separated by the gentle swell. Debris and wreckage were everywhere; including the remains of boats, upturned rafts, deck chairs, planks, lifebelts and various crates.

Smashed boats dangled vertically from their davits like toys. The floundering masses in the water faced a new danger as the great funnels descended on them; as the funnel tops reached the water, the sea gushed into their black chasms. A Mrs Guyer, wife of a Canadian clergyman, had a horrifying experience when she was caught by the inrush of water to one of the funnels and found herself being sucked in head first. As the funnel went under the waves, Mrs Guyer was miraculously belched out in a gush of soot and ash. She was subsequently plucked from the sea and, upon reaching Queenstown, was overjoyed to learn that her husband had also been rescued and was waiting ashore for her. Less fortunate swimmers were snagged by the funnel stays and dragged down with the ship; others were entangled on the twin wireless aerials strung high between the ship's masts. As the bow dipped to make its final death plunge, the stern rose high in the water and exposed the brass propellers which glinted in the sunlight. The engulfing seas made no distinction between the grimy stoker and the fashionable millionaire; the child that romped in the handsomely appointed first class suite and the unwashed urchin who played in steerage class were victims, sacrificed equally as they were snatched from innocent play.

The spot where the liner had been was marked by a plateau of turbulent water, boiling and gushing as it tossed bodies like corks in a maelstrom shrouded in smoke and steam. Then the water flattened and calmed and the smooth swell spread a glasslike finish over the tomb of the *Lusitania*. As the white faces of the dead drifted by, the living cried out in anguish for help, while some prayed in unemotional monotone. Overhead, the seagulls swooped and circled in a noisy requiem over the grave of the wonder ship, which had so held the world in awe at its launching a short eight years before.

Farmers and fishermen on nearby shores were first alerted to the *Lusitania*'s plight when they heard a series of explosions rumbling in from the sea. As they looked seaward in amazement, they saw the struggling *Lusitania* billowing clouds of black smoke and steam. The world was soon to learn of the catastrophe, as the ship's wireless operator tapped out a frantic Morse code message, '... *SOS ... come at once ... big list ... position ten miles southwest of Kinsale.*' Various ships in the vicinity quickly picked up the message which was intercepted as far away as Land's End. Almost immediately a second cry for help was transmitted '... *want assistance ... listing badly ...*', whereupon the *Lusitania*'s wireless fell silent, presumably from power failure. Admiral Coke of Queenstown reacted to the news by ordering all ships available to the scene of the disaster. Horror gripped the town as the shock news spread rapidly. A half dozen tugs steamed forth, followed by torpedo boats and a fleet of assorted trawlers. However, at only three miles distance, a small Manx fishing lugger, the *Wanderer,* was the craft nearest to the stricken *Lusitania*. The skipper, Captain

Ball, and his six-man crew had been casually watching the great liner pass by when they witnessed the explosions and the chaos that followed. The *Wanderer* had 800 mackerel on board and was just about to shoot its nets again when the tragedy unfolded. While aware that the big liner was in difficulty, they did not realise at first that it was the great *Lusitania*. The little twenty-one ton fishing boat, undeterred by the potential danger of a lurking submarine, made all possible sail and headed for the scene of the disaster. On arrival, she rescued 110 passengers from the first two lifeboats, and 50 or 60 from the next two. The *Wanderer,* now carrying over 160 occupants, was in grave danger of sinking and could not take another soul on board. However, the crew still persisted in their valiant efforts and took two more lifeboats in tow before heading for Kinsale. As the pitiful convoy left the scene, the crew busied themselves making tea and dispensing their meagre rations and clothing among the approximately 200 survivors. Many of the victims had broken limbs, and Captain Ball later stated that their plight was indescribable. The ship's single bottle of whiskey was distributed among the needy. Despite poor wind conditions, Captain Ball made it to within two miles of the Old Head of Kinsale when he was intercepted by the government tugboat, *Flying Fish*. The weary and shivering passengers, whose faces were stark with terror, were transferred for the final leg of their melancholy journey to Queenstown.

There were many acts of bravery and self-sacrifice as passengers helped each other to escape the terrible fate of drowning in the cold Irish sea.

Another fishing trawler, the *Dan O'Connell,* was also in the vicinity and rescued approximately eighteen survivors and sixty bodies from the sea. The survivors, who were said to be mostly women and children in a deplorable condition, were later transferred to the government tug, *Stormcock.* Only two days earlier, the *Dan O'Connell* had rescued the crew of another victim of the U-20, the schooner, *Earl of Lathom,* which was also sunk off the Old Head of Kinsale. Many of the exhausted and dripping survivors refused to take off their lifejackets in the rescue boats as they believed that the submarine was still stalking them with a view to finishing off its deadly work. The steamship *Heron* and two trawlers were assigned to gather up the dead. They returned to Queenstown with over 100 bodies, most of them women. All were taken to the three temporary morgues in the Town Hall. The vast majority of rescue boats took four to five hours to reach the scene; the only work left to do on arrival was to collect the floating corpses from the sea.

Queenstown became the town of the dead as the temporary morgues filled with bodies. The anguish, and sometimes anger, of the townspeople was aggravated at the sight of helpless, half-clad, soaked and shivering women struggling over the piers at Queenstown as they disembarked from the rescue boats. Some unfortunates held precious babes in arms, while others moaned for some lost soul. Dishevelled, white-faced men, some without clothing, formed part of this grim procession of humanity descending on Queenstown. The poignant grief was deepened by the sight of rows of bodies of babies and children as they lay, calm-faced like dolls, in the makeshift houses of death. Each newly arrived boat brought more dead to swell the ever-increasing numbers in the morgues. The tug *Polzee* arrived with sixteen dead, including three babies; the corpses were brought ashore on stretchers, while the sailors carried the three babies in their arms. The dispatches stated that the babies had retained a freshness and suppleness of life as if death had not been painful. As they came ashore, the officers on the pier saluted, civilians lifted their hats and women wept. One of the dead was little Betty Bretherton, who was turned over to her heartbroken mother who had miraculously survived the disaster.

The town opened its heart to the legions of devastated survivors who made their way ashore; hotels and private homes opened their doors to the bewildered victims. Surgeons, doctors and over a hundred nurses volunteered their services to aid the injured. Drapers, as well as private citizens, gave clothes and blankets. Stunned, and in many cases hysterical, the survivors thankfully accepted the hospitality of the townspeople. Many had been in the water for hours and nearly all had discarded as much clothing as possible to keep themselves afloat. Women came ashore wrapped in blankets, several wore men's clothing, nearly all were shoeless, and a great many were without socks. The locals and the authorities made every possible effort to alleviate their suffering. Many, having reached the safety of Queenstown, later died of exposure or their terrible injuries; morbid crowds surrounded the temporary morgues, where bodies awaited identification.

From the gloom and horror came stories of the unselfish heroism of those who went to martyrs' graves and sacrificed their lives for others. Some escaped death by a hair's breadth as they struggled to save lives. Alfred Vanderbilt, the multimillionaire sportsman, and his valet, showed great heroism as they tirelessly assisted women and children to the lifeboats. Though Vanderbilt could not swim, he gallantly took off his lifejacket and placed it around the body of a young woman. As he went to seek another lifejacket, the ship took its death plunge and he perished in a vortex of swirling water and hissing steam. Charles Frohman, the impresario, also showed remarkable courage when he handed his lifejacket to a lady in distress. He also perished with the ship and his floating body was later recovered from the sea to join the ranks of the dead.

A pretty nineteen-year-old Irish immigrant named Annie Kelly, from Galway, suffered a cruel irony when she made a round trip on the ill-fated *Lusitania*. Annie's boyfriend, William Murphy, had emigrated earlier to America and Annie hoped to join and marry him soon after her arrival. As an immigrant, she was obliged to undergo a medical examination before

An American victim of the *Lusitania*, shrouded
in the Stars and Stripes, is carried to a temporary
morgue in Queenstown.

entering America. The examination revealed a heart
defect which excluded Annie from entry because it
would limit her ability to earn a living. She was then
interned at Ellis Island for deportation as immigration

law decreed. In such instances, the ship that brought the immigrant to America was obliged to return that person at its own expense. This meant travelling in steerage for the return trip. When Annie's brother learned of her plight and confinement on Ellis Island, he took energetic steps to seek an exemption. He journeyed to Boston to petition the Mayor on the basis that he would personally assume all responsibility and care for Annie in the event of her health preventing her from working. He encountered one frustrating delay after another, but was eventually granted an exemption. He immediately left with all haste for New York only to discover that the *Lusitania* had departed just half an hour earlier. Annie perished in the disaster and her body was never found.

Elbert Hubbard, the author, publisher and lecturer, also went down with the ship. He was journeying to Europe to become a war correspondent. He had joked to friends, *'I may meet a mine or submarine over there, or I may hold friendly converse with a bullet in the trenches.'* During his last voyage, standing on the *Lusitania*'s deck, he made a prophetic statement to a reporter: *'Speaking from a strictly personal point of view, I would not mind if they did sink the ship. It might be a good thing for me. I would drown with her, and that's about the only way I could succeed in my ambition to get into the Hall of Fame. I'd be a regular hero and go right to the bottom.'* Elbert Hubbard had already condemned the German Kaiser with his vitriolic pen

Little Helen Smith lost both her parents and her baby sister Bessie on the *Lusitania*. She became the darling of the tragedy and is seen here with dolls given to her by the townspeople; too young to realise what had happened, she would tell curious bystanders in a melancholy voice, 'Mama and Papa are coming soon.'

for his policy of militarism which saw the devastation of Belgium. He issued a scathing indictment against him in his magazine, the *Philistine*. The article was titled 'Who lifted the lid off Hell?' and had the following to say, *'Bill Kaiser has a withered hand and a running ear, also he has a shrunken soul, and a mind that reeks of egomania. He is swollen like a drowned pup, with a pride that stinks. He never wrote a letter nor a message wherein he did not speak of God as if the Creator was waiting for him in the lobby. God is with us, God is destroying our enemies, God is giving us victories and I am accountable only to my conscience and God.'* Ironically it was Germany's policy of militarism that destined Hubbard and his writer wife to death on the last voyage of the *Lusitania*.

The entire Crompton family of father, mother and six children, ranging from six months to thirteen years, were lost on the *Lusitania*. Paul Crompton spent a considerable part of his life in the Orient, where he learned the Chinese language. The extent of his travels is illustrated by the birthplaces of his children. Stephen the eldest son, whose body was recovered, was born in Vladivostok in Eastern Russia. Catherine, aged twelve, was born in London, thirteen-year-old Alberta was born in South America and the other children, Romley aged nine, John aged five and baby Peter aged six months, were born in Philadelphia.

After a successful season of engagements in America, Hamish Mackay, the Scottish baritone and musician, was due to return to his wife and son in Edinburgh. He had performed at Carnegie Hall, New York, on 24 June 1914, at the celebration of the battle of Bannockburn. He had a great love of his native Scottish music, which he promoted at every opportunity. Hamish, who was exhausted and run down from his hectic tour, eagerly anticipated home and much-needed rest as he planned his return on the *Lusitania*. His wife, however, had a sense of foreboding about the ship and wrote to warn him to be sure to sail on the American liner *New York City* as the Germans would never dare torpedo a neutral passenger ship. She further warned him to take out American papers as soon as possible, so that Germans who might board his ship could not take him prisoner. However, the Monday after the *Lusitania* departed from New York, Mrs Mackay received a letter from her husband advising her that he intended to sail on the *Lusitania* and looked forward to meeting her in a few days. She was very apprehensive at receiving this news and spent the next few days in anxious anticipation of his safe arrival. Her worst fears were confirmed on the Friday evening, when she heard of the tragedy. A family friend, one Mr Angus, journeyed to Queenstown in a futile search for her husband. Having examined the morgues in vain, he interviewed many of the survivors, who recalled that his lost colleague had sung beautifully on Thursday evening at the ship's concert and promised to sing again on Friday. After his week long stay, Angus came to accept the worst and abandoned all hope of finding his friend alive.

In total, 1,198 lives were lost on the *Lusitania*. Behind each one there is a sad story to be told. One cannot imagine the last thoughts of the doomed and the dying. Only God can have known their agony of mind, their tortures of despair, their last fleeting memories of home and safety, their regrets for having ignored the last-minute warnings of the German Embassy, their concern for distant children or parents, the hopelessness in the realisation that the war visited them with an unjust death sentence. Of the drowned, 127 were Americans, 79 were children including 39 infants under the age of two years. Of the 1,198 lost victims, approximately 200 corpses were recovered from the sea. The remainder were never found. In August of the same year, a badly decomposed and bloated male corpse was washed up on the coast near Galway. From items of clothing on the body, it was identified as American and prepared for shipping to the United States on the Allan Liner *Hesperian*, which was ironically torpedoed by Schwieger in command of U-20. This tragic coincidence earned the macabre distinction of an American citizen being committed to the deep on two occasions by the same assailant.

Worldwide, anxious and distraught people poured into Cunard's offices seeking information about passengers and crew. Personal enquiries were supplemented by a steady shower of telegrams from all parts.

h the sight of moving coffins came the realisation that there were 1,000
e dead out in the chilly Atlantic. Wagons and horses were gathered from
ver County Cork to assist the hearses on funeral day. A procession of carts
mbled to ferry the dead to the old cemetery outside Queenstown; coffins
e draped in the Union Jack while ships anchored in the harbour lowered
their flags to half mast to show their respect.

The jingle of telephone bells played an accompaniment to the frantic efforts of overworked employees engaged in revising lists and answering questions. Clerks were obliged to double check their information before releasing it. First releases of messages were made at Cunard's head office in Liverpool. Most of the men and women who made enquiries for relatives or friends manifested their grief; some fainted, others became hysterical, tears streaming down their faces. Those who received good news sobbed with relief as they heard the name of a loved one read off the list of those saved. Some shouted names to clerks only to receive the ominous reply, 'not yet received'; this caused them to beg that the lists be re-checked or to ask if by chance it was a spelling error, as the name 'must be there'. Crowds lingered all day around Cunard offices in anticipation of revised lists which might end their nightmare.

On Monday, 10 May, three days after the sinking of the ship, the awful crime was marked by the passage of a funeral cortege through the streets of Queenstown. Reverently and mournfully the town paid full honours of the nation to the bodies of 140 men, women and children who lost their lives on the *Lusitania*. When the funeral started, people sensed the full horror of the tragedy as the long line of coffins slowly disappeared over the hill behind the town on their way to the graveyard. The bustle in the temporary morgues was replaced by an eerie silence as the dead made their final journey.

A brass band of the Royal Irish Infantry leads a two-mile cortege to the old Queenstown cemetery. Soldiers standing to attention lined both sides of the road and country folk stood on ditches and listened to the doleful strains of Chopin's *Funeral March*.

All shops and businesses closed for the day. The deathly silence that had descended on the town was broken only by the tolling of the great bells of St Colman's Cathedral and the dirges of the bands. Soldiers and sailors escorted the cortege to the cemetery in a quiet valley just outside the town. A company of British soldiers had dug three mass graves, each measuring 40 feet by 20, ready to receive the dead. The bodies of identified American dead, as well as those of some British first class cabin passengers, were not included in the Queenstown burials but rather embalmed and returned to their native countries for burial. When the first flag-draped coffin appeared, the chattering in the crowded thoroughfares stopped as if by signal. Men removed hats and women murmured devoutly in prayer. At St Colman's Cathedral, Bishop Browne of Cloyne presided at the requiem mass in the presence of Vice-Admiral Coke, representing the Admiralty. General Hill represented the army, and local authorities in the district were represented by their respective officials. After the celebration of Mass, the funeral procession began with the British Army band playing Chopin's *Funeral March*. Shutters of shops were erected, curtains of houses were drawn, and wheels of factories were stilled in silent respect. Soldiers lined both sides of the road and stood to attention as the funeral made its two-mile journey to the cemetery. Country folk stood on ditches and stone fences behind the soldiers. Those who had assembled at the graveyard first heard the notes of the funeral march and then the muffled sound of the drums; a moment later the sun flashed on the band's instruments far off, as the cortege came into sight. So long was the cortege that it took over an hour to pass. It was led by a major of the Royal Irish Infantry

A service at one of the three mass graves in the old Queenstown cemetery, two miles outside the town; as the last words of prayers were spoken, the muffled drums rolled and the hymn 'Abide with me' swelled forth.

and five members of the Irish constabulary; behind them a group of Protestant churchmen, followed by thirteen black-robed priests, each walking before a hearse. The mourners trudged at the rear and included many survivors of the catastrophe; members of the Cork Corporation were led by the Lord Mayor of

Cork. A party of naval officers and sailors arrived from ships anchored in the harbour; Bishop Browne rode in a carriage. Choir boys bearing incense burners stood beneath a group of tall elms at the graveside as Bishop Browne conducted the Catholic services and his colleague, the Reverend Archdeacon Daunt, conducted the Church of Ireland services. As the last words of the service were spoken, the muffled drums rolled and the hymn 'Abide With Me' swelled forth. Sailors, who had replaced the soldier pall bearers, lowered the coffins into the graves. Simultaneously, shovels sliced through the mounds of fresh earth and soil thudded down on to the coffins. At the conclusion of services, a firing-squad comprising soldiers as well as sailors fired a volley over the mass graves.

On 12 May, as searches of coves and inlets intensified, another twenty-nine bodies were recovered from the sea and brought ashore. The number of recovered dead was now 173 and continued to increase over the next few months as finds were made along the south and west coasts of Ireland. Each gruesome find brought back vivid memories of the tragedy. The anguish of that sad chapter in Queenstown's history is captured in a most elegant bronze monument that was later erected in the town to commemorate the mournful event.

Today, the mass graves of the *Lusitania* victims are marked by three large rough-hewn limestone rocks, with simple bronze plaques affixed. Another twenty-

The headstone of three-year-old Alfred Scott Witherbee bears the epitaph: 'A victim of the *Lusitania* foully murdered by Germany'.

eight individual *Lusitania* graves surround this tragic spot. Some are empty; they commemorate bodies never recovered from the chilly depths of the Atlantic. The mood and bitterness of that sad time is reflected in some of the inscriptions to be found in the old cemetery at Queenstown; the headstone to the three-year-old infant, Alfred Scott Witherbee, bears the epitaph, 'A victim of the *Lusitania* foully murdered by Germany', another headstone to Inez and George Ley Vernon, bears the epitaph 'Both young, beautiful

A headstone to the Vernon children bears the inscription: 'Both young beautiful and gifted'. Tragically, there were many children among the dead of the *Lusitania*.

One of three headstones marking the mass graves of the *Lusitania* dead in the Queenstown cemetery.

and gifted victims of the *Lusitania* crime'. The old graveyard is set on a hillside amid verdant valleys. The tall elms that once sheltered the incense-bearing altar boys have long since been superseded by yew trees that stand as silent sentinels to guard the dead. As the tall grass rustles in the breeze, the ghosts of the *Lusitania* dead seem to be at peace among the lichen-shrouded headstones; the tranquillity of their final haven little disturbed by the distant drone of motorway traffic, invisible and sonorous, like waves breaking on a far-off shore.

There are other graveyards dotted along the south and western coasts of Ireland that also remind us of the *Lusitania* dead. Church records indicate thirty-nine more bodies interred in remote churchyards. Five males are buried in Cork's Jewish cemetery; the infant Betty Bretherton is buried in the nun's cemetery at Blackrock Convent in Cork; two other passengers were buried at Cork's military barracks. Leaving Cork city, we find the resting place of two nightwatchmen in Kinsale's ancient cemetery of St Multose. Further west finds victims buried in cemeteries in Clonakilty, Skibbereen and Castletownbere. Tragically, bodies were recovered all along the coast, from Kerry, Galway and even County Mayo.

The memorial in Cob
formerly Queenstow
which remembers tho:
who so tragically diec
in the sinking of the
Lusitania.

TO THE MEMORY OF ALL WHO PERISHED BY
THE SINKING OF THE LUSITANIA MAY 7 1915
AND IN THE CAUSE OF UNIVERSAL AND
LASTING PEACE

LABORARE EST ORARE
WHO HELPED IN THE RESCUE GAVE AID AND COMFORT
TO THE SURVIVORS AND BURIED THE DEAD

8

The Sham Tribunals

THE *LUSITANIA* HAD BARELY slipped beneath the waves on that fine afternoon in May when accusation and counter accusation began to fly. The initial shock of disbelief was replaced by rage at what the world perceived to be the slaughter of 1,198 innocent lives. Germany alleged that an exploding cargo of munitions on the *Lusitania* was responsible for the rapid demise of the ship, and freely admitted from the outset that it had crippled the great liner but went on to stress that it launched only a single torpedo. A second explosion occurred shortly after the torpedo strike. Captain Schwieger noted this in his log and described it as an 'extraordinarily heavy detonation'. None of the *Lusitania* survivors appears to have timed the interval between the two explosions, but it was suggested that it was somewhere between half a minute and one minute. However, Lieutenant Scherb, the first officer on the U-20, stated that it was a fraction of a second after the torpedo blast. Scherb was also adamant that only one German submarine took part in the attack and not two, as the British had alleged. Britain countercharged that the *Lusitania* was an innocent passenger liner for which the Germans had laid a trap. Britain also denied Germany's allegation that the *Lusitania* was fitted out with guns and carrying Canadian troops and was therefore a legitimate target. Germany cited the illegal 'ramming orders'. Britain rejected all these allegations as groundless.

Questions were still raised, however, such as why did the Royal Navy not take steps to escort the great liner through the danger zone? Why did the ageing cruiser, HMS *Juno,* return to Queenstown and anchorage within hours of the *Lusitania's* passage outside that harbour? Was Captain Turner negligent in navigating his ship? Did he refuse to obey Admiralty instructions about course and speed? Did Turner disobey orders to zigzag as a way of outwitting the submarine? Did Germany not declare its intention to sink the *Lusitania* when it issued a warning notice in the American press on the same day that the liner departed from New York? Why were rescue boats turned away from Kinsale shortly after the disaster and forced to make the longer journey to Queenstown, despite the fact that some of the survivors were dying of hypothermia or in urgent need of medical attention for injuries sustained when the ship went down? No satisfactory answers to these questions have been forthcoming.

The first attempt to analyse the disaster occurred at the coroner's inquest held in the old Kinsale courthouse on 8 May 1915, the day after the disaster. Before the authorities had time to prevent rescue boats entering Kinsale, three male corpses and two female ones had been landed ashore in what was then a quaint old fishing town. Coroner John Horgan endeavoured to establish the cause of the five deaths when he convened a coroner's jury made up of local fishermen and shopkeepers. Captain Turner attended the inquest and testified that one torpedo had struck the ship and that the second explosion must have been internal. This evidence is very significant as it was given two days after the event and therefore the various details would be very fresh in Turner's mind. More significant, however, is the fact that Turner testified before Cunard, the Admiralty or the legal profession got to him. Coroner Horgan questioned Turner about navigation matters and asked him if he had received any special instructions as to the voyage. Turner replied that he had but was not at liberty to reveal them and referred the matter to the Admiralty. At the conclusion of testimony, the coroner expressed his sympathy to Captain Turner over the loss of his ship. He expressed his appreciation of Turner's bravery in the situation. In his verdict, Horgan charged the Emperor of Germany, the German government, and the officers of the submarine with wilful murder. As the inquest progressed, Britain's crown counsellor arrived from Queenstown to prevent Turner from testifying further to the Kinsale jury, but he arrived one hour too late as the inquest had closed.

In keeping with other great maritime disasters, the British Board of Trade was obliged to hold an enquiry to determine the circumstances and cause of the sinking of the *Lusitania*. Permission to hold the enquiry was granted by Churchill on 10 May 1915. However, permission was granted subject to the Admiralty controlling its scope and approving of the questions that might be asked. Many witnesses were screened before the trial and asked to write out drafts of their intended statements which resulted in many being rejected. It is reasonable to assume that there was a need to curb repetition in numerous statements, but there are also strong indications that statements against the government's interests would be rejected. The enquiry was chaired by Lord Mersey, the British forensic marine expert, who had presided over such past investigations as the loss of the *Empress of Ireland* and the *Titanic*. Two naval and two merchant officers attended as assessors.

Late in the evening of the disaster, 7 May, the Admiralty had already decided to make Captain Turner the scapegoat for the loss of his ship. Fisher, the First Sea Lord, wrote a memorandum to his colleagues before the trial, which stated: '*I hope*

Captain Turner will be arrested immediately after the enquiry, whatever the verdict.' Captain Webb of the Admiralty trade division stressed, in his own memorandum, the utmost importance of screening questions to be asked. He further warned that any failure to do so could have a most injurious effect on public confidence in the Admiralty. On 14 May, Churchill wrote his approval of Webb's memo and also suggested that the unfortunate Turner be *'pursued without check'.* Lord Mersey received a private letter from the Admiralty which stated: *'The government would consider it politically expedient if the captain of the* Lusitania *were promiscuously blamed for the accident.'*

It is useful at this stage to examine exactly what it was the Admiralty might wish to cover up at an enquiry. It was of paramount importance that the Admiralty conceal the existence of Room 40 and the fact that they were reading German ciphers. The intelligence gleaned by Room 40 was vital to the war effort and had to be protected at all costs in the interest of national security. Loss of this vital intelligence source might have meant the difference between victory or defeat for Britain.

The Admiralty needed to conceal their knowledge about the movements of the U-20 prior to 5 May when the submarine revealed itself by sinking the *Earl of Lathom* off Kinsale. Such foreknowledge might raise some very awkward questions as to why no escorts or protection were provided for the oncoming *Lusitania*. The inexplicable failure to warn Queenstown or Liverpool of the presence of the U-20 needed to be suppressed. Advocates of the conspiracy theory see this failure to pass on vital information as another move in Churchill's game-plan to embroil the *Lusitania* with a German submarine and thus bring America into the war. Alternatively, we can only attribute the failure to warn Queenstown to an intelligence blunder at Whitehall. Either way, the public might interpret this lapse as nothing short of a reckless disregard by the Admiralty for the safety of the *Lusitania* and its civilian passengers and crew.

The Admiralty also had good reason to cover up the fact that the *Lusitania* was shipping munitions and explosive substances, as this would embarrass neutral America. American law prevented the shipping of munitions or explosives on passenger liners leaving its ports. This law originated in a statute referred to as The Passenger Act which was first enacted in Congress in 1882 and subsequently amended at various times up to 1913. It stipulated that *'no vessel could legally sail with any explosives likely to endanger the health or lives of passengers or the safety of the vessel. For any violation of the provisions of this section the Master of the vessel shall be deemed guilty of a misdemeanor, and shall be fined a sum not exceeding $1,000 and be imprisoned for a period of not exceeding one year.'*

The statute further declared that '*if lives were lost as a result of an explosion due to fraud, neglect, connivance, misconduct or violation of the law, then those knowingly involved were guilty of manslaughter and liable to a fine of $10,000 and/or confinement at hard labor for a period of not more than ten years.*'

If munitions or explosive substances were proved to be on board the *Lusitania* at the time of her loss, then the Collector of Customs for the port of New York, Dudley Field Malone, could conceivably face a charge of manslaughter for having failed in his duty to uphold American law. His immediate superior William McAdoo, the Secretary of the Treasury, would also face serious consequences. Shock waves from such a scandal would reverberate all the way to President Wilson's office and could jeopardise his administration.

Presumably these issues were foremost in the minds of Churchill and the Admiralty when the Mersey enquiry convened on 15 June, five weeks after the Kinsale enquiry. Churchill's career as First Lord of the Admiralty was in tatters and his days in Whitehall were numbered as he walked the thin ice of political survival. Public awareness of the Admiralty's dithering in the *Lusitania* incident would be sufficient to send him crashing into an abyss of defeat.

An impressive array of legal talent attended the Mersey enquiry to represent the various parties concerned, such as the government, the Board of Trade, the Cunard company, the passengers, the Canadian government, as well as the crew members and engineers of the ill-fated liner.

Two of the most eminent lawyers of the day, Sir Edward Carson, Attorney General, and F.E. Smith, the Solicitor General, defended the government's case. Turner did not stand much chance against their brutal cross-examination. The Admiralty's intention from the start appeared to be one of moving the spotlight away from itself and on to Turner, but not in such an obvious way that it might let Germany off the hook.

Just five days before the Mersey hearing commenced, further limits were imposed on the testimony when a statute was enacted in parliament on 10 June 1915 under Britain's Defence of the Realm Act (DORA), making it a treasonable offence for a British subject to divulge information concerning the carriage of munitions or placement of guns on any ship of Britain or her Empire. Cunard produced a letter from the Admiralty in court stating that all relevant directives concerning the navigation of the *Lusitania* and all relevant wireless messages had been supplied to the court and that total disclosure of Turner's orders would be detrimental to the state. To prevent disclosure of the Admiralty's secret instructions to merchant ships, evidence regarding the liner's navigation was heard in camera. As already mentioned, these instructions related to the illegal misuse of flags, the ramming order, and the order to refuse a submarine challenge to halt and search.

These various instructions were in breach of guidelines codified at The Hague in earlier years, and referred to as Cruiser Rules. It is surprising that Germany, which was aware of the Admiralty's secret instructions, did not cite them in justifying their foul deed. A merchant ship intending to ram an enemy ship legally assumed the status of a hostile or belligerent ship, and as such was not eligible for protection under Cruiser Rules. Captain Turner had received the secret instructions prior to his ill-fated voyage, probably in February, when Churchill first conceived the strategy. Germany could have argued that it had no safe attack alternative to firing a torpedo without warning on what it perceived to be a ship with hostile intent.

On 12 May 1918, the White Star liner *Olympic* sighted the German submarine U-103 on the surface of the English Channel at night. Without further ado, the liner charged at the submarine at full speed. The resultant collision ripped the submarine apart and sent it plunging to a watery grave. One can only speculate as to what action Turner would have taken if the U-20 had surfaced and allowed the crew and passengers time to disembark before completing the *Lusitania*'s destruction. It is most likely that Captain Turner would have carried out his secret instructions from the Admiralty, and rammed the U-20, thus reversing the tragedy and committing Schwieger and his officers to the deep off the Old Head of Kinsale. Merchant ships that were successful in ramming and sinking German submarines received very substantial cash rewards from the government for doing so.

Captain Richard Webb, Director of Admiralty Trade Division, prepared the Admiralty's case for the hearing. As Director of Trade, Webb's duty was to warn merchant shipping when danger threatened; this warning would usually be accompanied by recommended countermeasures to safeguard such shipping. Webb was the person who should have warned the *Lusitania* but chose to remain silent for some inexplicable reason. After the loss of the *Lusitania,* prying eyes began to fall on the Admiralty which remained inactive throughout the affair. Webb now found it necessary to invent certain warnings and instructions in his attempt to create a very busy role for the Admiralty, and he examined and considered what orders or instructions Turner was known to have had in his possession. In his examination, he took excerpts from printed Admiralty directives dating from 3 November 1914 to 26 April 1915. Some of these directives were already in place for seven months before the disaster. Webb further examined wireless messages broadcast between 6 May and the day of the sinking, 7 May. The instructions examined by Webb were general instructions to all ships and not directed specifically at the *Lusitania,* as Webb was later to claim. Webb then extracted out-of-context passages from the various directives, which were later used to accuse Captain Turner of disobeying them. Webb's concoction was submitted to Churchill on 14 May in the form of a memorandum titled *Lusitania: Consideration of Master's Actions.*

Webb's memorandum subsequently had its date adjusted back to 8 May, and with some minor revisions to text and title, was passed as the prosecutor's brief against Turner at the in camera Mersey hearing. The doctored instructions were passed to the court as the supposedly unabridged copies of the Admiralty's directives. Thus was mixed the whitewash for the sham tribunal and the scapegoating of the hapless Captain Turner.

Webb's gossamer-thin zigzag allegations do not stand up to scrutiny. He charged that Turner disobeyed orders to adopt a zigzag course. This practice of zig-zagging was routinely adopted by Royal Navy ships in submarine-infested waters. In essence, the practice means that a ship alters its course at irregular intervals to make it more difficult for a submarine to gain a favourable attack position. As in nature, many a fleeing animal has often eluded its attacker by the use of this technique. This practice was not extended for use by the Merchant Navy until after the *Lusitania* incident. Captain Turner did not receive this order and was very confused when accused of disobeying it. He conceded that 'he must have seen it' but misunderstood the order, as it sounded very different when read out by the court.

Turner was also accused of disobeying an order to avoid usual trade routes. This out of context instruction was lifted from an Admiralty directive issued in November 1914 to all ships and intended to help merchant ships steer clear of German warships in the North Atlantic and not the south coast of Ireland.

Another abridged instruction on Webb's list included the order to make port at dawn and have lifeboats swung out. Had the full text of this telegram been read out to the court, the Admiralty's case would have collapsed immediately as the instruction contained the lethal and top secret ramming orders to merchant ships as well as the instruction relating to submarines' visit and search. This telegram was first introduced on 10 February 1915, three months before the *Lusitania* disaster and was issued in response to Germany giving the world advance notice of its intention to implement its U-boat blockade on 18 February 1915. Turner was also accused in court of disobeying a wireless order to steer a mid-channel course. Firstly, there is no channel off the Old Head of Kinsale. Secondly, the word 'channel' is defined in the dictionary as a narrow region of sea between two land masses. If one faces due south from the Old Head of Kinsale, the nearest opposing land mass is the coast of Spain. Webb extracted his mid-channel accusation from an instruction relating to merchant shipping movement in the English Channel and Dover Straits region.

The original telegram states: *'Between South Foreland and Folkestone keep within two miles of shore and pass between the two light vessels, take Liverpool pilot at bar, avoid headlands, pass harbours at full speed, steer mid-channel course.'*

The full telegram was broadcast nightly just after midnight as a general warning to all ships in the English Channel. Webb also suppressed the fact that this was a routine message transmitted nightly to merchant ships since 22 March, over seven-and-a-half weeks before the *Lusitania* met her fate.

Turner could not have disobeyed specific instructions, as alleged in Webb's memorandum, as he had received no such instructions. Those he received were of a general nature, vague in their content, inaccurate, out of date, and in stark contrast to the very precise instructions sent to the HMS *Orion, Gloucester* and *Jupiter* when faced with the same threat.

Another issue, the second mystery explosion, drew a lot of attention as it was noted by almost every survivor. This was potentially embarrassing as it might lend credence to German claims of exploding munitions in the forward part of the ship. This was explained in the court, which found that two torpedoes had struck the ship. One had exploded between number one and two funnels, and the other had exploded between number three and four funnels. If one is to accept this conclusion, it seems very odd that the ship sank so rapidly at the prow when so much damage was inflicted at the stern. Mersey also decreed that no other substance exploded or ignited. Any further questions about the second mystery explosion were thus discouraged. Mersey further found that several U-boats had lain in wait for the *Lusitania*. In his somewhat surprising verdict considering the evidence presented against Turner, Mersey exonerated Captain Turner and the Cunard company, he heaped the highest of praise on the Admiralty for their diligence in collecting all the information available likely to affect the *Lusitania,* and praised them for their most anxious care and thoughtfulness throughout the affair. One wonders what words of praise Mersey might have heaped on the Admiralty had they provided an escort of Royal Navy ships for the *Lusitania,* as they had done in the past, or if they had informed it about the loss of the *Centurion, Candidate* and *Earl of Lathom,* or the U-20's close encounter off Queenstown Harbour with the steamship *Cayo Romano,* or indeed the following day's near-miss with the White Star liner *Arabic*. Mersey's judgement commended the crew for its discipline and competence. The opposite is true, however, in the case of those crew members who were launching the lifeboats, which was a fiasco.

Mersey finally decreed that the whole blame for the cruel destruction of life in this catastrophe must rest solely with those who plotted and with those who committed the crime. When the verdict was made public, many of the survivors received it in stunned disbelief. Captain Turner left the court, a bewildered villain who was seen to be negligent and reckless in handling his ship. He was just another expendable pawn in the higher game of cynical chess played out in the corridors of the Admiralty. Like many before him, Turner had learned another of life's cruel lessons: that a court of law is not necessarily a court of justice.

However, Captain Turner's day in court did not end with the Mersey tribunal. In the aftermath of the *Lusitania* disaster, a number of personal claims and lawsuits were filed against the Cunard company on the premise that they had operated their liner negligently. Accusations ranged from allegations of shipping munitions, to leaving portholes open and thus creating undue flooding. Further accusations were also voiced about leaking and defective lifeboats and Captain Turner's mishandling of his ship in a known submarine zone. Few actions were brought in Britain as most were initiated in the United States, where escalating claims soon exceeded $6 million. Fearing ruin and bankruptcy, Cunard petitioned the American federal court to limit their liability. In preparation for the American hearing, a commission was set up in London in 1917 to gather evidence. Evidence previously presented to the open sessions of the 1915 Mersey tribunal was entered into the New York record with certain stipulations.

In complying with these stipulations, the petitioners inadvertently waived their rights to challenge the validity of the evidence. This sleight-of-hand enabled Cunard to prevent conflicting new evidence being heard on matters already adjudicated by Lord Mersey, such as the erroneous two-torpedo conclusion, the incorrectly stated points of impact well aft of the bridge and the denial that a second explosion occurred in the forward part of the ship. The DORA statute, which was enforced at the Mersey hearing, was also entered into the New York record by Cunard's lawyers and imposed further constraints on evidence. Cunard must have realised their case would not be enhanced by presenting a captain who had been accused of negligence, incompetence and glaring disobedience of orders at the Mersey court only three years previously. Towards the end of 1916, Turner was given the captaincy of the Cunard liner *Ivernia* and in 1917 the *Mauretania*. During this time, he was also promoted to commodore of the Cunard shipping line. The bewildered captain must have been somewhat perplexed about the sudden fall and subsequent rise of his career in a mere two years. These sudden and unexpected promotions must have gone some way to help obscure past allegations of incompetence and recklessness.

Judge Julius Mayer presided over the American enquiry, and the navigation of the ship became a very contentious issue. Cunard's refusal or inability to provide a complete account of the Admiralty's instructions to Captain Turner caused claimants to motion unsuccessfully for a stay of verdict until after the war when the missing directives would become available. While admitting that the absence of the directives was vexing, Judge Mayer declared that he failed to see how their contents could significantly alter his findings. Had Cunard's officers attempted to reveal their contents to the court, they might well have found themselves guilty of treason under the DORA statute.

The *Lusitania* sank at a very acute angle, by the bow, with a near-vertical list to starboard. To account for this sequence of events, the head of the Massachusetts School of Naval Architecture and Marine Engineering, William Hogvaard, attended the hearing. Hogvaard presented the results of a study he had made to determine what events could cause the ship to sink in the manner it did.

Assessing the effect on the ship's stability if any two boiler rooms or their adjacent coal bunkers flooded as a result of an explosion, rupturing their common transverse bulkhead, he contended that the ship would not have sunk from that alone. If struck between the third and fourth funnels, the *Lusitania* would have trimmed slightly by the stern. If struck between the second and third funnels, she would have settled practically parallel to herself. If struck between the second and first funnels, she would have trimmed considerably by the bow with a starboard list of fifteen degrees. At this point in his statement, Hogvaard was denied permission to continue and give his findings if the ship had been struck further forward. Instead, Hogvaard asserted that the *Lusitania*'s sinking, as described at an angle of thirty degrees by the bow, would not be consistent with flooding of number one boiler room, and could only occur if damage was inflicted to the *Lusitania*'s bow so that water gradually found its way to the forward part of the ship and filled up completely. Hogvaard's evidence to Judge Mayer was held in camera and sealed. Mayer excluded this expert testimony from consideration, adjudging that in time of war it would be detrimental to the public interest.

Ships leaving New York in 1915 were obliged to comply with the usual Customs regulations required to clear port. A manifest of goods on the ship was turned over to the Customs authorities for inspection and approval. This list of cargo items was accompanied by a signed and sworn oath declaring that the manifest presented contained *'a full, just, and true account of all goods, wares and merchandise which were laden or to be laden aboard the ship.'*

US Customs depended on the sworn manifest to determine if there were illegal goods on board the ship. Only if explosives or other illegal goods were listed, or if suspicion was aroused, would the ship's cargo be physically examined. On 30 April 1915, the

Lusitania cleared the port of New York on a single page manifest. This 'just and true account of all goods laden' made no mention of the fact that the *Lusitania's* cargo also included five thousand 3.3 inch shrapnel shells, 4.2 million Remington rifle cartridges, 3,200 percussion fuses and 46 tons of aluminium powder. This manifest submitted by the *Lusitania* to the New York collector of Customs was even made out in the name of the wrong captain, one who had left the ship in March. This was Captain Dow who, incidentally, was born in Ballinspittle, a village only fifteen miles from the *Lusitania's* final resting place off the Old Head of Kinsale.

The full *Lusitania* manifest, which was hand-written and ran to twenty-four pages, gave a more detailed account of the cargo. This was presented to the New York Customs on 5 May, five days after she had departed from New York. The usual master's oath was blank, unsigned and unwitnessed. The twenty-four page supplementary manifest included descriptions of the munitions. If the New York Customs had disapproved of these new revelations, one wonders what action they could have taken as the liner was now within one day of making landfall with Ireland. Ethics aside, the United States shipped enormous quantities of munitions and guns to Britain on a daily basis during the war. The voracious appetite of the war in Europe brought unprecedented prosperity to the American economy, with records being set in all sectors, especially shipbuilding, aircraft and munitions manufacture. The Cunard company routinely shipped munitions on their liners in conjunction with other shipping lines; fast liners meant speedy deliveries of very urgently-needed war materials. At first, companies like Cunard and White Star resisted mixing passengers with munitions until forced to do so by government pressure. There is absolutely no doubt that the US port authorities turned a blind eye to such practices.

One of the exhibits at the New York hearing was a typewritten version of the *Lusitania*'s original twenty-four page manifest. This contained some subtle differences from the original; its date adjusted to imply no late filing; the word munitions was no longer used at this hearing and was substituted by the more sanitised reference to 'government stores'. The 194 cases of potentially explosive aluminium powder listed on the original manifest were also deleted from the typed version. It was this deletion that stimulated John Light to search for a reason during his exhaustive researches. His Sherlock Holmes' intuition bore fruit when he eventually discovered the highly explosive nature of this commodity. The only other major deletion from the manifest was 138 cases of copper and brass tubes. Unlike the aluminium powder, this was not a sensitive item of court evidence, and there appears to be no explanation for its deletion.

At the time of the New York hearing, America itself was at war with Germany and anti-German sentiment was running high, with no shortage of propaganda to fuel the hysteria. In many respects, Judge Mayer's conclusions were duplicated by those of the 1915 Mersey trial in England. Both courts had been provided with the same Admiralty directives on which to draw their conclusions.

Mayer agreed with the erroneous two-torpedo theory and also agreed that no other explosion occurred. With all the horror of war now in the public domain, Germany could hardly expect an impartial judgement from a country with which it was at war. In his summation, Mayer exonerated the Cunard company, Captain Turner and the officers of the ship from condemnation as he heaped the whole blame for the disaster on Germany. Cunard must have heaved a sigh of relief at the decision, as it exempted them from addressing ruinous financial claims. Claimants would now have to wait until the war was ended to pursue their claims with the real culprit, which was identified as Germany by Judge Mayer.

On 6 February 1916, Germany accepted full responsibility for the loss of American lives on the *Lusitania,* and the rights of Americans to claim indemnity. Germany subsequently honoured American compensation claims, paying them their dues, ten years after the tragedy, in 1925.

9

Munitions and Explosives

AFTER THE SINKING of the *Lusitania,* the general public were surprised to learn that a portion of its cargo included munitions and explosive substances. Included in the munitions were 18-pounder shrapnel shells, Remington rifle cartridges and percussion fuses. Germany alleged it was exploding munitions that caused the *Lusitania* to sink so rapidly. Schwieger, the commander of the U-20, noted in his log that an extraordinarily heavy detonation occurred shortly after his single torpedo exploded under the bridge of the liner and even speculated on his log as to the possible cause.

This was not the first time the *Lusitania* shipped munitions; an examination of her cargo manifest for her penultimate voyage reveals a very similar shipment. White Star liners and others also assisted in transporting munitions to feed the insatiable demands of war. During the early stages of the hostilities, Britain repeatedly underestimated the enormous amount of munitions required daily for her troops and was obliged to rely heavily on the United States' armaments manufacturer, Bethlehem Steel Corporation, to fill the void. Britain's shell production in 1915 was 22,000 units per day, compared to 100,000 by France and 250,000 by Germany. This situation was largely attributed to trade union intransigence in not allowing the dilution of skilled labour in the interest of increased production. Such union rules could only be modified after long negotiation for which there was no time. Strikes occurred at British munitions factories which further exacerbated the shell crisis and in October 1915, a law was passed to curb the drinking of alcohol which was said to be seriously affecting munitions production and shipyard work. David Lloyd George spoke out about the evils of drink on 3 May 1915, and allegations about heavy drinking by arms workers gave the government cause to consider imposing tougher new measures to curb alcohol abuse. Lloyd George, as Chancellor of the Exchequer, described Britain's three main enemies as Germany, Austria and drink. A government advertisement asking for views on prohibition brought 70,000 letters in favour. Whatever were the true reasons for delays, Lord Kitchener complained constantly about slow deliveries of arms and supplies to troops on the Western Front.

In the spring of 1915, the grave munitions crisis led to a public outcry initiated by Colonel Repington, the military correspondent of *The Times*. After consultation with Sir John French, *The Times* threw its full weight into a fearless campaign which culminated in the establishment of a Ministry of Munitions under Lloyd George, to co-ordinate and develop both the supply and manufacture of war material. The effect of the press campaign was of incalculable value in rousing the people and clearing obstructions. Churchill intervened personally with the unions to the mutual advantage of both sides.

On the *Lusitania*'s last voyage, her forward cargo hatches contained 1,250 cases of 3.3-inch shrapnel shells with a total weight of 52 tons. Each box contained four shells making up a total quantity of 5,000 shells. When examining the waybills and the shipping invoice for this consignment, one will notice the notation 'filled'. At first glance this implies shrapnel filled with explosive and therefore live shells. To date none has been recovered from the wreck to prove or disprove that there were live shells, but various clues on the invoice hint at empty shells that could not have been detonated by an exploding torpedo. Shrapnel shells are sometimes described as air-burst shells and were especially suited to trench warfare. In essence a shrapnel shell is a projectile containing a load of bullets encapsulated in resin. The projectile is described as a full round when attached to its brass cartridge case and fitted with a timing fuse in its nose. Shortly before firing a shrapnel shell from a field gun, the gunner adjusts the setting on the timed fuse to cause the shell to explode in mid-flight as it passes over enemy trenches. Such an exploding shell would then rain down its lethal load of bullets in all directions with a killing or maiming radius of 250 yards. Shrapnel or air-burst shells were first conceived out of necessity when it was realised that rifles were largely useless in countering an enemy underground or safeguarded by a trench system. The shipping of shrapnel on the *Lusitania* became a very contentious issue and was examined at length at the New York Limits hearing in 1918. Mr George Streuble, the manager of the Bethlehem Steel Munitions factory that made the shells, was summoned to attend as a sworn witness. Streuble swore under oath that the shrapnel shells did not contain any explosive whatsoever, nor were they fitted with fuses or attached to their brass cartridge cases. They were, however, filled with resin and bullets and capped with a transport plug to prevent the ingress of moisture. Streuble even produced a cutaway sample for the court to explain the mechanics of shrapnel shells. There is no reason to doubt his testimony when other considerations are made. The consignment of shrapnel shells on the *Lusitania*'s last voyage was destined for the Royal Arsenal at Woolwich for use by the British Army. At Woolwich, incomplete imported ammunition would be filled with its explosive charge and have its transport plug substituted by a brass timer fuse.

Had the *Lusitania's* shells been complete, they would have been shipped directly to an ammunition depot in Britain. This would allow normal stock control and the issuing of shells in rotation according to date of manufacture. The invoice gives us another clue when we examine the weight of the shells. Each box of four is described as having a weight of 72 pounds. Therefore, each shell weighed 18 pounds indicating that they were projectiles only. If the shells on board the *Lusitania* had been full rounds with their brass cartridge cases attached, then each unit would have weighed 22 pounds and 14 ounces. As inert objects of steel, resin and bullets, the shrapnel on the *Lusitania* could not have ignited, or exploded to hasten the demise of the liner.

Before Streuble left the witness stand he was cross-examined about another Bethlehem Steel consignment shipped on the *Lusitania,* namely eighteen cases said to contain 3,240 brass percussion fuses. These fuses did not relate in any way to the shrapnel just mentioned and were designed for an entirely different shell, namely 4.7-inch high explosive type. In testimony, Streuble revealed that the said fuses were not in fact manufactured by his company but rather by a subcontractor, the Hartford Screw Company of Connecticut. However, they bore the initials BSC for Bethlehem Steel Corporation. Again Streuble swore under oath that the percussion fuses were not filled with explosive and contained nothing but steel and brass parts. Streuble's evidence was inadvertently reinforced by a chance find in 1982. A team of divers from the company Oceaneering Contractors were exploring the ship's strong-room in the aft portion of the *Lusitania* when they stumbled across the wooden crates containing the fuses. One member of the diving team, Frank Mulcahy from Cork, kindly loaned this author two fuses for further examination. The fuses were set on the jaws of a lathe and drilled for inspection. The chamber on the fuse designed to hold its explosive charge was found to be empty, as Streuble had claimed in his evidence.

Unlike the empty shrapnel projectiles and brass percussion fuses, a consignment of 4,200,000 Remington rifle cartridges on the *Lusitania* was live. Germany was fully aware of the intended purpose of these cartridges, namely to shoot German soldiers. One analyst calculated that if only one cartridge in every hundred of the *Lusitania*'s shipment killed a German soldier at the Front, it would represent a staggering 42,000 dead, not to mention the potential carnage of the shrapnel shipment. Germany saw the loss of the *Lusitania* as an event that saved thousands of German lives.

The *Lusitania*'s sizeable cartridge consignment was contained in 4,200 boxes whose loading aboard the ship was supervised by Remington's arms traffic manager, Frank Monaghan. So numerous were the boxes that they were used as dunnage (packing) for other cargo throughout the forward cargo hatches. Long before the *Lusitania* disaster, concern was expressed about shipping sports ammunition on passenger trains and ocean liners. Extensive tests had been carried out to establish if such ammunition could explode en masse. These tests included placing cartridges in fires as well as dropping them from tall buildings and jarring their contents. Tests showed beyond doubt that the cartridges would not detonate en masse from this treatment and if placed in fires would burn off harmlessly. They were thus exempted from the stipulations of the Carriage of Passenger Act and deemed safe to include with liners carrying passengers. Remington produced first-hand sworn evidence of the validity of their safety tests at the Limits hearing. The findings of the court ruled out the cartridges as a contributory factor in the loss of the liner.

What then sank the *Lusitania*? The second mystery explosion that occurred shortly after Schwieger's first torpedo has stimulated the minds of historians and experts to the extent of studying the ship's manifest for clues. The hand-written, twenty-four page manifest lists over 200 categories of goods. Listed items such as the munitions and cartridges attract immediate attention when going through the list for possible clues; however, in the light of what has been said, we can eliminate these from our list.

Almost camouflaged in the obscurity of the mundane items is a listing of aluminium in the cargo manifest. This substantial shipment occupied 1,190 cubic feet of space and consisted of 144 cases and 50 barrels, weighing 46 tons in total. Each case and barrel was individually stamped with a number sequence that ran consecutively throughout the shipment. The method of marking certain items of cargo by numbers was adopted by the British War Office as it was considered desirable to avoid revealing their true contents by naming the container. On the manifest the stated numbers are prefixed by the notation <NA>. The initials refer to the manufacturer, North Aluminium, and the diamond brackets around the initials indicate that the shipment was destined for army use. Other items on the *Lusitania*'s manifest are bracketed in a rectangle indicating that they were intended for navy use. The cases and barrels contained very fine aluminium powder and were destined for the Royal Laboratory, the explosives manufacturing section of the Woolwich Arsenal. Aluminium powder was used extensively at Woolwich in the manufacture of all nitrate-based explosives during the First World War. The United States produced 50 per cent of the world's aluminium powder and, as such, was Britain's major source of this commodity. In 1915, Britain imported it at rates exceeding 400 tons per month. Woolwich used aluminium powder mainly in the production of ammonal explosive, a very popular filling at the time for shells, grenades and various bombs.

Aluminium fine powder has some unusual properties. If heated beyond 30 °C and brought into contact with water, it liberates hydrogen gas freely. Fires in industry, where aluminium powder is present, may not be extinguished by water; to do so would have disastrous consequences from igniting hydrogen. Aluminium is also explosive in yet another way: when aluminium powder is disturbed to create a dust cloud, it can readily be detonated by a source of ignition such as a spark or fire to cause a violent explosion. Dust-cloud hazard is well known in industry; even common household substances such as flour, very fine sugar and coal dust are explosive under the right conditions. Numerous chemical and industrial products and some metals are also explosive. The severity of such explosions varies widely depending on the substance being used. This property is defined by scientists as KST value. On a scale of one to ten, aluminium is a very volatile number ten compared to coal dust, flour or sugar which rate at number three on the same scale. When dust-cloud explosions occur in industry, they tend to create further local clouds which initiate secondary explosions in rapid succession, creating a deep rumbling sound. Numerous survivors of the *Lusitania* described the second explosion as a 'deep rumbling sound' in the forward part of the ship. The aluminium powder on the *Lusitania* was stored in cargo hatch number two, just forward of the bridge and adjacent to where the torpedo struck the ship. The late

John Light's lifetime study led him to theorise that the single torpedo, which struck the *Lusitania,* exploded on the bulkhead dividing cargo hatch number two from the ship's only transverse coal bunker. The resultant explosion disturbed its aluminium powder cargo to cause a dust cloud which exploded as a result of fires caused by the torpedo. A rumbling series of explosions that followed blew the bottom out of the ship. Sceptics may argue that if such an explosion occurred, it should be simultaneous to the torpedo blast and not spaced approximately a minute after, as seems to have been the case. Another characteristic of aluminium powder in cloud form is that it will not explode if the mixture of cloud particles is too dense or too lean. However, a dense cloud would soon thin as particles settled back to ground and thus bring the mixture within the explosive parameters required for ignition. John Light attributed the rapid sinking of the liner in eighteen minutes and the loss of almost 1,198 lives to the second explosion that occurred on the *Lusitania.* At the time of the explosion, a large proportion of seamen on the *Lusitania* were hauling out suitcases in the forward baggage hatch just above where the aluminium was stored. Sadly, not a man survived. However, there were survivors from all three working boiler rooms, including number one boiler room which was separated by a transverse coal bunker from the compartment where the aluminium was stored. Cargo hatch number two was the very area of the *Lusitania's* foreship that Professor Hogvaard was prevented from referring to when offering his findings to the New York Limits hearing.

I, the author, fabricated a dust-cloud test explosion chamber in order to witness at first hand the effect of exploding a teaspoonful of aluminium fine powder. A one litre steel chamber was modified for the experiment by adding a set of sparking probes to create a source of ignition as well as a means of inducing a puff of compressed air to disturb the fine powder under test. A lid was tightly clamped to the chamber and doubled as a weak link or rupture disc. Each test produced a shotgun-like bang as the rupture disc disintegrated in a blinding white flash which sent a plume of white smoke rapidly skyward. Many survivors of the *Lusitania* described a cloud of white smoke high above the wireless aerials after the second explosion occurred on the *Lusitania*. Scientific data indicates that pressures as high as seven bars can build up in a confined compartment as a result of an aluminium powder explosion. This pressure is vastly greater than that required to rip a ship asunder in the event of an internal explosion. In continued tests, explosions were initiated over an average range of temperatures down to minus 3 °C and in a range of conditions from dry to very humid. Not a single misfire occurred throughout the tests. While these 'exploding teaspoon' experiments can be regarded as the work of a non-qualified amateur, it is nevertheless

To witness first hand the explosive nature of aluminium fine powder, the author (*pictured*) initiates a controlled dust-cloud explosion using a level teaspoon of aluminium powder in a test chamber.

frightening to consider the effect of 46 tons of the same substance exploding in cargo hatch number two of the *Lusitania*.

In summing up, one can only conclude that the second explosion that rocked the *Lusitania* was nothing more sinister than an industrial accident. The inclusion of a lethal aluminium consignment on a ship that carried passengers may have been a heedless oversight or a lapse in upgrading safety regulations to cater for the additional hazard potential of an exploding torpedo or mine in a wartime situation. When one considers that the shrapnel shells and percussion fuses were both empty, it must indicate that the authorities adhered, if loosely, to United States Federal law in relation to the Carriage of Passengers Act, referred to elsewhere in this book. We have no proof that the bottom blew out of the ship as John Light theorised, because the remains of the once-proud liner are lying over the damage, thus preventing inspection by diver or remotely-operated camera. Doctor Ballard and his team from National Geographic photographed the *Lusitania* extensively in 1993 and found the port side of the ship adjacent to the torpedo-strike area to be fully intact, and not with a large tear running from main deck to keel as John Light had concluded. When we consider that Light used a breathing mixture of compressed air when he made his forty-two dives to the *Lusitania* in the 1960s, the accuracy of his observations would have been weighed against a drowsy haze of nitrogen narcosis which he must have suffered at these depths. This condition is unavoidable to air-breathing divers working at great depth. However, a vital piece of circumstantial evidence prevents us dismissing Light's conclusions that a large piece blew out of the bottom of the *Lusitania*. The single largest item of cargo included in the liner's ill-fated voyage was a 6,000-cubic-foot consignment of fur pelts. These pelts somehow escaped from the sunken liner and floated ashore in huge quantities where they were eagerly gathered up by local fishermen and sold to the Cork furrier family of Messrs Rohu Limited. This company devoted some time to drying out the pelts before re-selling them to the British Army who had bought them in the first instance. Could these pelts have exited through a large hole in the starboard side of the *Lusitania*?

Another riddle presents itself by the existence of an anomaly on the seabed a few hundred yards off the wreck of the *Lusitania*. This is presumed to be wreckage and is well known to Kinsale fishermen as a place to be avoided for fear of losing fishing gear and nets. This may prove to be the wreckage of a French trawler from times past, or even another casualty of the First World War. What if it is the 58-ton consignment of shrapnel shells which may have fallen through the same hole from which the fur pelts exited? Further visits to the wreck may produce some answers to these tantalising questions, as well as offering tangible proof that the shrapnel shells were not filled with explosive.

10

The Aftermath

AS THE DUST SETTLED and the *Lusitania* dead were laid to rest, a flame of indignation and anti-German sentiment swept to the four corners of the earth. The gathering momentum of the 'Hate the Hun campaign' made the Kaiser realise that the sinking of the *Lusitania* was a propaganda disaster for Germany. Violent incidents flared up throughout Britain and America, and other countries to a lesser degree. The rounding up of German spies and suspects, which had commenced in 1911 after the Agadir crisis, was intensified. Some German citizens were forced to flee from Britain as they feared for their safety, while others were interned. To be a suspect made life very uncomfortable indeed. Even in Ireland's Cork city, Thompson's Bakery was obliged to publish announcements in local newspapers denying that they employed confectioners of German or Austrian extraction. Rumour and innuendo implied the opposite to be true and was proving damaging to their business. Even owners of dogs with German-sounding names were looked on in a dubious light. In Liverpool, the home port of many of the drowned firemen and crew members, German shops were attacked and burnt by rioting mobs and enraged widows as they rampaged through the city to avenge their dead.

Further afield in Canada, the city of Victoria was placed under martial law as mobs plundered and destroyed German-owned shops and businesses, making it necessary to call in reinforcements of troops from nearby Vancouver to restore order.

London joined in the anti-German demonstrations as the wrecking continued. All German-owned restaurants in the Strand were closed and placed under police protection. Within a few days, over a hundred German or Austrian-owned shops in London were destroyed. Many were forced to display a notice which declared, 'This is not a German shop. God save the King'. Some citizens in fear for their lives had to seek police protection, while violent disorder was reported in scores of other English cities as people demanded that all Germans and Austro-Hungarians be interned. The ringleaders of these disorders, who were prosecuted, were shown leniency by the courts who warned that any repeated action would merit rigorous punishment.

In Washington, controversy erupted at the National Capital Horse Show. A group of young girls and women stationed themselves around the city and about the grounds of the Horse Show. They had hoped to reap a rich harvest for the day as they sold flowers for charity; the flowers were artificial and made from starched cambric, dyed blue and built around a wire to represent a cornflower. Unknown to the enthusiastic young ladies, the cornflower or *Kaiserblume* was also the national flower of Germany. When a member of the crowd pointed out the German connection with the cornflower, a great commotion broke out as many people refused to wear the flower of a murderer and ripped them from their buttonholes and stamped them in the mud; many left the Horse Show in protest. The flower sellers were advised to stop selling the flowers and to leave the grounds.

Newspaper bulletin boards were thronged with crowds eager to discover the latest news, as many stated that America now had no option but to wage war against Germany. Walter Hinze Page, the American ambassador in London, declared that, '*The United States must declare war or forfeit European respect.*'

Germany hailed the sinking of the *Lusitania,* with its cargo of munitions, as a great success and an event that saved thousands of German lives. There were triumphal editorials written, as well as poems and postcards, and in Munich, a private medal maker named Karl Goetz struck a medal to commemorate the event. The medal was dated 5 May 1915; the *Lusitania* was sunk on 7 May. This was held by British authorities as absolute proof that the sinking was planned in Berlin and that the medals had been struck to commemorate the deed before it had been committed, although the plan misfired to the extent of the liner being sunk two days later than scheduled. In fact, Karl Goetz did not make his medal until August 1915, three months after the loss of the *Lusitania*. In a letter to The American Friends Service Committee in Frankfurt in 1921, Goetz stated that the incorrect date on the medal was a printing error on his part and taken by him from a newspaper account which had erred on the date.

British propaganda immediately recognised the potential of these medals to whip up anti-German sentiment and authorised huge quantities to be manufactured by a London firm and distributed worldwide. The London fakes were presented in an attractive gift box with a picture of the *Lusitania* on its cover. The box contained inflammatory literature to show the barbarous nature of the German people. The crude fakes proved to be a powerful instrument of Allied propaganda.

By November 1916 Karl Goetz, the medal maker, stated that 180 *Lusitania* medals were in existence. The bad press caused by the British fake medals prompted Baron von Speidel of the German War Office in Munich to ban Karl Goetz from manufacturing further medals, and stated that all available pieces were to be confiscated under martial law. This may explain the extreme rarity of these medals today. In various letters after the war, Karl Goetz was adamant that his satirical medal was not intended as gloating over the slaughter of the innocents on the *Lusitania* but rather to censure the unscrupulous Cunard company for negligence by mingling innocent passengers with munitions of war. Goetz later attempted to undo some of the damage caused by the misinterpretation of his medal when he issued yet another satirical piece lampooning British propaganda in Sweden. The Swedish *Lusitania* medal failed dismally to dilute anti-German sentiment.

The *Lusitania* atrocity had the effect of stimulating recruitment and various colour posters were printed depicting the sinking ship and drowning victims. These posters urged men to 'enlist and avenge the *Lusitania*'. Lifebelts and even a raft were produced at recruitment meetings to help whip up enthusiasm for enlistment.

Having sunk the great Cunarder, Schwieger returned home several days later to a tumultuous welcome. Britain had been humbled by the loss of her 'Greyhound of the Seas'. Perfidious Albion had been brought down a peg and perhaps would now spare some thought for the starving civilian population of Germany who were enduring a ruthless hunger blockade imposed by Britain. Many Germans saw the *Lusitania* as a fully armed reserve cruiser shipping ammunition to its enemy. After all, the *Lusitania* was on the Navy list and classed as Royal Navy Reserve Merchant Cruiser; she was also included in Jane's Fighting Ships

A German cartoon portrays the *Lusitania* as a floating crate of munitions expecting rights to steam through a war-zone with impunity because it had American passengers on board. Concealed guns and shells protrude from canvas coverings. The name has been adjusted to read *Explositania* to remind the public that the great liner was also a gun-runner. American President Wilson rides on the crate.

List and in 1913, plans were freely published showing her intended wartime emplacement of twelve 6-inch guns. In essence, she was more warship than liner and should be treated accordingly. The loss of life of so many civilians was regrettable but the misguided passengers had been warned and chose to ignore these warnings. Churchill and the Admiralty had been totally reckless in using innocent women and children as human shields to protect a vital munitions cargo. If they had any concern for the liner, why was an escort of destroyers not sent out to bring her to safety? The Cunard company had been greedy and irresponsible in its policy of mixing passengers and munitions on the same ship. The *Lusitania* also had orders to ram German submarines on sight and therefore was a belligerent ship with hostile intent. The Kaiser was soon to feel the effect of the anti-German backlash and the subsequent alienation of his country by America, as he realised that the sinking of the ship was a colossal blunder by Germany. The massacre, which included the loss of 127 American lives, seriously undermined the goodwill of Americans and other neutrals toward Germany. Within days, a major diplomatic controversy arose between the United States and Germany. Like Captain Turner, Walter Schwieger was soon scapegoated as his superiors isolated themselves from his brutal deed.

President Wilson of the United States demanded an immediate cessation of the U-boat war against commerce and one month later, the Kaiser relented under pressure and implemented a ban on his U-boats from attacking passenger liners in the future. An endless flurry of notes and exchanges took place between the American and German governments. Germany apologised 'with comment' to the United States for the loss of her citizens but maintained an inflexible stance throughout as it defended its own reasons for the incident. Analysis of the intricacies of the diplomatic duel between both governments are outside the scope of this book; suffice it to say that the various notes sent to and fro achieved little more than paving the path to war for America.

However, the remorseless Schwieger continued to wage war against enemy merchant shipping in his U-20 and appeared to have paid scant attention to the Kaiser's ban on attacking passenger liners. Four months after the *Lusitania* incident he stalked, and attacked by torpedo, the Allan liner, *Hesperian,* which he encountered 85 miles southwest of Fastnet, on 4 September 1915. The *Hesperian* had 653 passengers and crew aboard and miraculously only 32 lost their lives; this may be attributed to the fact that the liner, which was struck amidships, took several hours to sink which allowed ample time for passengers and crew to take to the lifeboats. In the three days that followed the loss of the *Hesperian,* Walter Schwieger sank five more steamers: the *Duro*, the *Rea*, the *Dictator*, the *Bordeaux* and *Caroni*. Only a month earlier, a fellow traveller of Schwieger's, Commander Schneider in the U-24, torpedoed and sank the White Star liner *Arabic* off the Old Head of Kinsale. This was the same ship that narrowly escaped the clutches of the U-20 on 6 May, one day before it sank the *Lusitania*. The *Arabic* had a total complement of 434 passengers and crew aboard, and 44 of this number, including American lives, were lost. Again America was enraged and this rage was soon to be fuelled by the loss of the *Hesperian*. One year and one day after the sinking of the *Lusitania,* the now notorious Schwieger happened upon another White Star liner, the *Cymric,* 140 miles west of Fastnet. The U-boat commander again flouted the Kaiser's ban by launching three torpedoes at the *Cymric,* which sank with a loss of only 6 lives out of 110 crew members. Fortunately, the liner carried no passengers on her moribund voyage. Both U-boat commanders were reprimanded by their superiors but offered a tissue of excuses in defence of their actions, ranging from mistaken identity to a belief that at least one liner was acting in a hostile manner by attempting to ram the U-24. Intense pressure from America after the *Arabic* and *Hesperian* incidents caused Germany to dispatch yet another note assuring them that the orders banning U-boat attacks on liners had now been made so stringent that a future recurrence of such an attack would be impossible. The new and more stringent ban remained in place throughout most of 1916.

The crucible of war cast three unlikely characters together and would forever inextricably link the names of Churchill, Turner and Schwieger with the story of the *Lusitania*.

Schwieger, the young submarine commander, did not survive the Great War and by 1918 his life was over, entombed in his steel casket, the U-88, at the bottom of the North Sea; very little is known about his pre-war life. However, it is known that, as he returned to Germany in 1916 having completed a routine patrol in western waters, he responded to a wireless call for help from the U-30 which had suffered diesel engine failure while patrolling twenty-five miles west of Bergen, in Norway. The two submarines eventually met up and proceeded to Bovsbjeg on the Jutland peninsula. As they neared their destination, fog descended and blinded both commanders and resulted in their submarines running aground on a sandbank. Vice-Admiral Scheer of the Imperial German Navy arranged assistance by dispatching the battle cruiser *Moltke* and a powerful squadron of destroyers to re-float the stranded U-boats. This was surely a reversal of attitudes from the early war days of 1914 when German Naval Commanders sneered with disdain on the lowly submarines and their crews whom they regarded as little better than insects. British Intelligence became aware of the salvage operation from wireless intercepts and duly alerted their submarine J-l which was patrolling in the area.

Commander Lawrence of the J-l had surprise on his side as he managed to manoeuvre his craft into a favourable attack position and launch four torpedoes at the German ships. One English torpedo struck the *Kurfürst* while another struck the *Kronprinz*. The wounded battleships did not sink, and limped back into port for repairs. The Kaiser reprimanded Admiral Scheer for recklessly exposing such valuable battleships by relegating them to a minor salvage operation.

The U-30 was re-floated after the salvage attempt but the U-20 stubbornly refused to budge and was subsequently scuttled and blown up to prevent her falling into enemy hands. Her damaged remains were abandoned on the sandbank until after the war when the U-20 was finally removed in 1925, as it posed a hazard to shipping. After the sandbank incident, Walter Schwieger was given command of the more modern and larger U-88, which was soon to become his tomb; his career ended abruptly on 5 September 1917, as he departed from Germany at the start of another mission, and unknowingly ran into an Allied minefield in the vicinity of Horns Reef off Jutland. The U-88 struck a mine which caused a colossal explosion and sent the U-boat plunging to a watery grave with all hands. Another U-boat commander accompanying Schwieger witnessed the explosion and thought at first that the U-88's torpedoes had exploded in their tubes. It was only later that he learned of the minefield. When the smoke and vapour eventually cleared, only a large oil slick and scattered wreckage marked Schwieger's resting place and that of his entombed colleagues. The thirty-four-year-old U-boat commander, who had cherished danger so much, had finally perished at his own game; and some would say poetic justice had been done. Had he survived the war, he would surely have been tried by the Allies as a war criminal.

Captain Turner had also reached a watershed in his career and was sixty-one years old when the Horns Reef mine sent Schwieger plunging to eternity. Turner, who was the son of a Liverpool sea captain, was born in 1856. He went to sea as a deck boy at the age of thirteen on the sailing ship, *White Star*. Life 'before the mast' was not for the fainthearted. At the outset of a voyage nimble-footed sailors were obliged to swarm up the rigging, and out along the spars as they unrolled canvas sails to form great white wings; others manned the windlass winch and set about hauling up the great anchors. As grunting men leaned on the capstan bars, a shantyman sang a rhythmic tune to coordinate their efforts. The clanking sound of the windlass told them that the dripping anchors were slowly inching their way up the ship's sides. As the sails caught the breeze, the ship would slowly gather momentum and presented a majestic sight to watchers on the shore as it seemed to wing its way in graceful silence to romance and adventure. The reality to those on board was starkly different, as a hellish voyage was getting under way. The ship's captain was lord paramount and ruled with iron discipline. One captain boasted that he would make sailors or mincemeat of his men if they showed the slightest signs of insubordination or laziness. Work on a sailing ship was endless as gangs of men heaved on rigging, adjusted stays and shrouds, tightened slack lines or loosened excessively taut ones; others were sent aloft into the rigging to work the sails. They climbed up ratlines and made their way out along spars with nothing more than a precarious foot-rope to stand on. Then, no matter how hard the wind blew or how stiff the rain-drenched sails might be, they had to grasp at canvas and shake it out or reef it according to the captain's orders. Working at these dizzying heights was a fearful experience for the novice sailor. A sudden slip or loss of balance could send him plunging into the seas far below or crashing down on deck to sudden death. Each rope in a numberless thicket of rigging had a specific purpose and required the sailor's intimate knowledge of its function. Sometimes sailors who had reefed sail aloft had barely regained the decks when a change of wind would send them scurrying back up the towering masts to undo the work they had just completed. Sailing through the southern hemisphere in winter's icy grip added greatly to the discomfort and danger. In Antarctic latitudes, water was near freezing point. Fog and mist would sometimes be superseded by howling gales which would bring alternate blasts of snow, hail or sleet. Mountainous seas would spring up and send the ship pitching from side to side with its yardarms almost dipping in the ocean. Crewmen still had to carry out their perilous duty on high, with numbed hands that could barely grip the freezing and stubborn canvas. Some fell into the sea, never to be seen again. Frostbite and chilblains were a new misery and those who were taken ill often died days later in their bunks.

When fair weather returned, there was less terrifying work to be done. The duty of 'holystoning', or rubbing the decks clean with a block of sandstone was endless. This back-breaking work was carried out on hands and knees. A bucket of icy water would regularly flush the deck and send its chilly sensations up through the feet of barefoot scrubbers. Those who dallied in their task could expect the mate's lash to come crashing down on their backs. Ropes required constant attention as they were repaired, spliced, knotted, tarred and served. Leaky decks were caulked with hemp and tar and damaged sails were repaired. Idleness was never tolerated and those not needed aloft were set to scraping, varnishing, painting, greasing or picking oakum for the caulkers. When fresh provisions were used up, the crew had to resort to a monotonous diet of salted beef and pork and hard bread or biscuits. Voyages were typically of three to four months duration.

This was the life chosen by the lad, Turner, as he sailed down the Mersey to make his maiden voyage on board the sailing ship *White Star,* bound for Aden via the Cape of Good Hope and the Roaring Forties. In his wildest dreams he could never have envisaged the era of the four-funnel liners of the future, let alone aspire to captaining such floating palaces as the *Lusitania*. In his apprenticeship before the mast, he worked on such sailing ships as *War Spirit, Thunderbolt* and *Royal George*. In 1878, he went to steam as third officer in Cunard's Mediterranean fleet. After two years, he resigned from steam and returned to his first love, sailing ships. In 1883, he again changed his mind and returned to Cunard. In that same year he leapt into Liverpool dock in freezing winter conditions to rescue a drowning boy and was subsequently awarded the Shipwreck and Humane Society's Medal for bravery. Turner's first steam command was the *Aleppo* in 1902. Over the course of the next ten years he commanded most of the notable steamers of the Cunard fleet such as the *Carpathia, Ivernia, Umbria, Caronia, Carmania, Lusitania* and *Mauretania*; he was awarded the South African Transport Medal for services rendered while on the *Umbria*. In 1911, he performed yet another mid-winter rescue while crossing the Atlantic on the *Mauretania*. During the crossing, he spotted a group of lifeboats drifting on the high seas; the boats were laden with survivors from the British steamer *West Point,* which had caught fire and had to be abandoned when the ship became an inferno. The rescue earned Turner an illuminated testimonial from the Shipwreck and Humane Society. Throughout Turner's career he continued to accumulate accolades and in 1913, King George V made him an honorary Commander in the Royal Navy Reserve. In June 1914, Turner was appointed captain of Cunard's latest and largest luxury liner, the *Aquitania*. On 1 August in the same year, the Admiralty drafted the *Aquitania* for duty as an armed merchant cruiser and within a week installed twelve 6-inch guns about her decks as well as ammunition magazines and a fire control system. During this period, operational responsibility shifted to a regular Royal Navy captain, and Turner assumed the role of Cunard's chief officer on board. The *Lusitania* and *Mauretania* were similarly drafted but later rejected, because the envisaged costs in running such ships would outweigh their usefulness as armed merchant cruisers (AMCs). The newly gunned *Aquitania* joined Cruiser Force E which was responsible for protecting merchant shipping in the North Atlantic, west of Ireland. Turner was also a member of the executive council of the Mercantile Marine Service Association.

In January 1915, Captain Turner was in charge of the passenger liner *Transylvania* when he was forced to make a run from a marauding submarine. Drastic measures were required and Turner gave orders to the engine room to put on all steam possible. After the hour, the steamer reached its best ever speed of eighteen knots. The lights were doused and the ship blacked-out as she throbbed under the strain of driving her engines far in excess of her design speed.

Turner's strategy paid off as he eventually distanced himself from his pursuer and made for the shelter of Queenstown. He was said to be an intrepid sailor and had constantly braved mines, torpedoes and submarines throughout his career. The loss of the *Lusitania* put the unfortunate captain on the world stage through the world's press.

Fate had one more card to deal to Captain Turner before the war ended. On New Year's Day in 1917, he was in command of the Cunard liner *Ivernia* which was bound for Alexandria and was carrying about 2,400 troops made up of the Argyle & Sutherland Highlanders, Royal Scots Fusiliers, Rifle Brigade and Yeomanry. The *Ivernia* had been escorted by a destroyer since it departed Marseilles on 28 December and Captain Turner was given a specific course and instructions by the Admiralty. New Year's Day 1917 found the *Ivernia* fifty-eight miles southeast of Cape Matapan as it steamed eastward in heavy seas. Turner was on deck and the morning sun was shining brightly on his starboard side when he noticed the white streak of a torpedo-wake approaching his vessel. In an instant, it struck under the funnel and the resultant explosion ruptured steam lines and disabled the engines. Commander Steinbauer of the submarine UB-47 had discharged the lethal torpedo. Fortunately, all hands were on deck at the time and the launching of the lifeboats proceeded in an orderly fashion. As the ship sank, eighty-five troops of the ranks were drowned as well as thirty-four crew members, including the ship's surgeon and chief engineer. Some of the victims died at the hands of the escorting destroyer, which, in the confusion, unfortunately collided with one of the laden lifeboats. At the time of the collision, the destroyer had been manoeuvring to locate the submarine. Two steam trawlers in the escort assisted in transferring the survivors and injured to Crete. The loss of the *Ivernia* earned Turner the unusual distinction of having two great liners torpedoed from under him and he survived both to tell the tale.

Before the war ended, Captain Turner was promoted to Commodore of the Cunard Line and eventually decorated with an OBE for his services to king and country. Turner retired to a neat little cottage by the sea, near Liverpool, with Mabel Every who had been his lifelong companion and housekeeper from 1908 until his death in 1933. Turner died a bitter man and resented his scapegoating over the *Lusitania* incident at the hands of the Admiralty.

The *Lusitania* disaster also etched a benchmark on Churchill's career. Unlike Captain Turner, the great Winston Churchill was a journalist, soldier, politician, statesman, war leader, grand strategist and Intelligence wizard, who came from an aristocratic background. Yet he was half-American, as his Brooklyn-born mother was the daughter of a New York lawyer and financier. In 1895, Churchill graduated with distinction from Sandhurst Military Academy and was commissioned as Second Lieutenant in the Fourth Hussars cavalry regiment. In his early years, he served a dual role of soldier and war correspondent. Adventure for Churchill first started in November 1895 when he sailed into Havana's harbour in Cuba; here he experienced the first thrill of warfare and also discovered the delights of cigars the size of 'broom handles', rum cocktails and afternoon siestas. The Havana cigar was to become his lifelong trademark. Guerrilla warfare was raging as Cuba strove to shake off centuries-old Spanish rule. Churchill reported on this war as a frontline soldier in the thick of the smoke and gunfire as he accompanied the Spanish troops to battle. Before leaving England, he signed up with *The London Daily Graphic* to publish his dispatches and received accreditation from the Spanish authorities. Finally, he was briefed in London by Colonel Edward Chapman, the director of military intelligence and veteran of past wars. Chapman urged Churchill to include the duty of amateur spy in his Cuban mission and gave him maps and instructions to guide him in his task. In Cuba, he marched against the enemy, was shot at by guerrillas and witnessed violent deaths. On his twenty-first birthday, a sniper's bullet felled the horse behind him. Churchill marvelled that a few thousand Cuban rebels under their general, Gomez, could pin down a Spanish army 250,000 strong. He noted that the enemy was 'everywhere and nowhere'. Guerrilla intelligence was of the highest order as they had the sympathy of the local people; rebels would break out to burn houses, blow up railways or capture Spanish forts and then fade back into the impenetrable jungle. This lesson in history was not wasted on Churchill, who applied the same tactics to the Balkans during the Second World War. In 1940, he set up a secret wartime agency known as SOE (Special Operations Executive) to create and wage subversive war behind enemy lines in Europe.

In the summer of 1897, Afghan rebels rose in revolt in the northwest frontier of British-controlled India. A punitive expeditionary force was sent against the rebels and Churchill made all haste to join them. Before long, he was once again in the thick of the action; on this occasion, he reported for the *Daily Telegraph* and *Allahabad Pioneer.*

In 1898, Churchill found himself at war in the Sudan as he reported for the *Morning Post.* On this occasion he joined Kitchener's army for the battle of Omdurman. There was much to report, with appalling scenes of carnage. After the battle, heaps of bodies lay festering in the desert sun while the dying and wounded pleaded for help and water. Churchill attributed Kitchener's victory to the high quality of intelligence provided by the Egyptian Army.

In 1899, war broke out between Britain and the Boers in South Africa. Immediately Churchill sailed for Cape Town. At this stage in his rapidly soaring career, he had resigned his army commission and had his eyes firmly fixed on Parliament. In the meantime, he was obliged to honour his contract with the *Morning Post* as he made his way to Natal and Ladysmith, where British troops had been surrounded by the advancing Boers. As Churchill travelled to Ladysmith, Boer saboteurs derailed some carriages from his train and subsequently imprisoned Churchill and his colleagues in Pretoria, the capital of the enemy Transvaal. In collaboration with two friends, an escape attempt was planned but only Churchill succeeded in scaling the high walls and escaping to freedom. Without maps, food or water, he made his way across 300 miles of enemy territory to the Portuguese East African border. At night, he navigated by the stars and cadged lifts by jumping on and off passing goods-trains. By now, the Boers had put a price on his head and on one occasion he was obliged to hide down a mine to evade capture. If caught behind enemy lines, he could be tried and shot as an officer of the British Army. His safe arrival back in Durban was greeted with great joy and the jubilant crowds carried Churchill shoulder high through the streets. At twenty-six years old, he was a celebrity, more eager than ever to embark on a political career. Over the next ten years his rapid climb to the top of British politics left observers breathless. Churchill's lifelong fascination with the 'secret war' and the world of intelligence was to stand him in good stead as the Great War loomed large on the horizon of 1914.

At the outset of war, he devoted great energy to setting up the new Intelligence division in Whitehall known unofficially as Room 40. This goose laid many golden eggs for Churchill by betraying the movements of the German Navy and U-boat arm, by revealing a 'Casement' plot to smuggle a shipload of German guns to Ireland in anticipation of the 1916 Rising, and bringing America into the war in 1917 by leaking the contents of the Zimmerman telegram.

In January 1915, Britain began to search for a new war strategy that might break the stalemate in the trenches and hasten the journey to victory. Turkey seemed a likely area to achieve fresh victories. On 5 January, hard-pressed Russia had appealed to Lord Kitchener, the Secretary of State for War, to apply military pressure on Turkey and thus bring relief to the Russian Army by halting Turkish advances. Russia's huge armies found their fighting efficiency greatly impaired by lack of ammunition. The most practicable route by which supplies could be delivered to Russia was via the Dardanelles. However, this route was sealed by Turkey's entry into the war in October 1914, on Germany's side. Kitchener suggested that an Anglo-French attack on the Dardanelles could drive out the Turks and simultaneously help Russia. Victory in the Dardanelles would give the Anglo-French forces access to the Danube. The initial strategy was to use ships only and Churchill, as First Lord of the Admiralty, gave his enthusiastic and wholehearted support to the plan. He was convinced that British warships could easily blast their way through the narrow Turkish waterways and penetrate to the Sea of Marmara. Enormous hopes of success were entertained by the British War Council; some members believed that the Turkish garrisons on the Gallipoli Peninsula would drop their guns and flee at the sight of the world's mightiest navy outside their doorstep. In the euphoria of imminent victory, territorial gains and the sharing of spoils after conquest were even discussed.

At the outset of war, Britain had cast a loop of steel around Germany's Western Front in the form of the 'Hunger Blockade'. Victory in the Dardanelles would enable that loop to be closed and form a noose of strangulation on the Eastern Front. However, Churchill and his colleagues in the war council had seriously underestimated Turkish military strength and bravery. As soon as Turkey was threatened, she took energetic steps to strengthen her defences; six Turkish divisions moved into the peninsula. Turkish labour gangs erected barbed wire, dug trenches, erected machine-gun emplacements and reinforced existing defences. Germany, which had so much to lose by a British victory, threw her might behind Turkey and sent in 500 officers and men to help the Turks in their preparations. The Germans also sent in aircraft and dispatched submarines and minelayers to repulse the attack from the sea. Some major ships of the Royal and French Navies had been lost to submarine and mine. Combined military and naval assaults by the Allies did not have the desired effect and Churchill's envisaged 'easy victory' turned into a bloodbath and humiliating defeat as each month rolled by. Injury and loss of life had been caused to over a 500,000 men and the Allied troops were finally evacuated in January 1916. Today, monuments and war graves dominate the Gallipoli Peninsula as they commemorate the dead of British, Irish, French, Australian, New Zealand and Turkish soldiers.

After the Dardanelles fiasco, Churchill's political career was in tatters and as the *Lusitania* dead were being buried at Queenstown, he was fired from his post as First Lord of the Admiralty. After seven years at the centre of power he was out in the cold. He had no secretaries, no executive power, no ministerial responsibility and he was without the army of bureaucrats at his command. Nor did he have any access to the brainchild he had created in the form of the Secret Intelligence Service in Whitehall. Aged forty, his world had seemed to end. He had little alternative but to accept the lesser, if not humiliating, role offered to him and from January to May 1916, Churchill reappeared on the Western Front in command of the Sixth Royal Fusiliers in Belgium.

Driven by restless energy, Churchill found he had spare time on his hands and added painting to his many skills. As a soldier in Flanders in 1916, he made his first clumsy attempts at portraying what life was like living under a hail of shells and gunfire in the trenches. He had no formal training in painting and had never held a brush in his hand before his demotion from the Admiralty. Soon his confidence and skills grew as he broadened his range to include landscapes and portraits. In 1921, as Colonial Secretary, he attended a conference in Cairo and found time to paint the Pyramids of the Nile and a panoramic view of Jerusalem. In the same year, he exhibited his pictures in a Paris gallery under the pseudonym Charles Morin. Who would ever have guessed that they were viewing the works of Britain's busiest politician? Many of Britain's distinguished painters were only too eager to teach Churchill; one of them, Sir John Lavery, even offered him his studio, as well as giving him much valuable advice on technique and composition. John Lavery and his wife Hazel had been close friends of Churchill's one-time arch enemy, the Irish freedom fighter Michael Collins. Lavery had painted a portrait of Collins who always insisted on facing the door when he sat. Hazel Lavery's portrait graced Ireland's currency by appearing on the pound note after the Free State was founded. Hazel Lavery, who observed that Churchill painted very cautiously and in a hesitant manner, urged him to 'loosen up' and 'let go'. He should treat paint like his political enemies, 'splash into turpentine, wallop into blue and white' with a big brush, and 'make a frantic flourish on the palette, fierce strokes and slashes on the canvas'.

This was the encouragement he had wanted to hear. From then on he never looked back, as he realised the importance of audacity and spontaneity in painting. Churchill devoted most of his time to painting between the years 1930–39 when his career was in the political doldrums. In all, he produced over 500 pictures.

During the uneasy peace of the 1920s, the multi-talented Churchill wrote a personal history of the Great War. The book, titled *The World Crisis,* was published in 1923. In it he praised the Admiralty's resolute but unheeded efforts to bring the *Lusitania* safely through the danger zone, and emphasised Captain Turner's glaring disregard for orders. In making these statements, Churchill attempted to pass off fiction as historical fact. Throughout his life he penned at least eleven books with twelve appended volumes. In 1953, when Churchill won the Nobel prize for literature, some believed that the honour reflected more the quality of the man than his writing abilities.

The peace that followed the 1914–18 war brought new worries and anxieties to Churchill's mind. Stalin's Russia and spreading communism posed threats to peace and stability. Churchill saw Russia as a potential future invader who might some day bomb England's cities from the air as Germany had already attempted to do in the Great War. These mythical attacks could be coordinated by spies and subversives already planted in Britain. Spy-mania once again tormented

Churchill's mind as he focused his thoughts on post-war Germany, which had failed to honour the crushing conditions imposed on it by the Armistice and Treaty of Versailles. An unknown corporal named Hitler, who had received the Iron Cross for his bravery in the trenches of the Great War, did not see Germany as a defeated nation; after all, no foreign army had set foot on her soil throughout the war. Instead, he saw his country as one let down by its own people and especially those he wished to portray as enemies such as the government of Berlin and its alleged allies, Jewish financiers and Marxist subversives. Hitler blamed Germany's economic collapse on these imagined enemies of the state, from within, and this became the main theme of his numerous anti-government rallies. Germany secretly flouted bans and controls imposed on its armaments industry, and began to re-build its war machine. The war to end all wars did not serve its purpose and a shaky peace barely survived the next twenty years, when Europe was once more ablaze as the Second World War descended on the continent.

Once more Churchill rose from the political ashes to fulfil his destiny of reaching the summit of his career when he became Prime Minister of Britain in May 1940, just in time to give his country heroic leadership against the might of Hitler's Germany. In 1940, Britain once again faced defeat when Churchill seized an old and familiar weapon, the secret service, and fashioned it to meet new conditions of war.

Room 40 was superseded by Bletchley Park as the new Intelligence division which did much valuable work, and was a major factor in Britain's sweep to victory in 1945. The end of the Second World War did not restore tranquillity to Churchill's mind, as Europe entered the era of the Cold War and a Europe divided by the Iron Curtain. The secret war of intelligence now absorbed most of Churchill's energy; this was the murky realm of cloak-and-dagger work, spying, dirty tricks, and the toppling of regimes hostile to British and American interests. The world needed to 'keep its eye on Russia' and both Churchill and his American counterparts authorised spy plane missions deep into Soviet territory to photograph and glean vital intelligence on the military strength of 'the evil Empire'. Early 1960 found the retired Churchill and his wife Clementine planning a Baltic cruise as guests of Ari Onassis on his yacht *Christina*. The highlight of the planned trip was a visit to Leningrad which Clementine had last admired in 1945. However, a new incident in the 'Secret War' undid his plans; the American high altitude spy plane, U-2 and its pilot Gary Powers, were shot down over Russia. The failed reconnaissance mission precipitated a new crisis between Krushchev's Russia and the West. Cooling relations between both sides forced Churchill to cancel his visit.

Churchill had witnessed the rise and fall of the Empire before his death in 1965 at the age of ninety. The Queen led the nation in mourning for Britain's greatest statesman and the man who contributed so much to the survival of the free world. The royal families of Europe, as well as representatives of 110 nations, attended his state funeral in St Paul's Cathedral. For three days after his death, Sir Winston lay in state in Westminster Hall in the heart of the Houses of Parliament. As hundreds of thousands of mourners filed past his coffin, live television coverage relayed the event to an audience of over 350 million worldwide. Tributes poured in from all quarters. 'What he did will never die,' said President Johnson. 'In the war drama he was the greatest,' said De Gaulle. 'The indefatigable champion of freedom,' said the Pope. The most moving tributes came from the House of Commons, where he had sat for sixty years. Harold Wilson recalled his stormy career – the slaughter on the Afghan plains, his cavalry charge in the desert heat of Omdurman, the sound of horses' hooves thundering over the veldt during the Boer war in Africa, the guns of Gallipoli and Flanders, Dunkirk and the Normandy beaches, the wailing of air raid sirens as angst-ridden Londoners ran for cover, the threat of Nazi Germany – 'There is a stillness,' said Wilson, 'and in that stillness each has his memories.' After four days of homage, Churchill's remains were laid to rest in a village churchyard near his ancestral home at Blenheim Palace, Oxfordshire. The endless adventure that had been Churchill's life was now ended, leaving a great void in the spirit of his nation.

11

The Mysteries Unravel

WHEN THE GREAT WAR erupted on Britain in 1914, her merchant ship owners discovered that they could not insure their ships. For obvious reasons, Lloyds was reluctant to insure ships that might, at any moment, be committed to the bottom of the Atlantic as a result of enemy action. Numerous categories of merchant ships, from the majestic liner to the rusty tramp-steamer, were required for government use to transport huge quantities of armaments, spare parts, non-ferrous metals, munitions, explosives and other supplies acquired from the United States to feed the insatiable war machine. Great liners were needed to ferry troops to theatres of operation or serve as hospital ships to cater for the wounded. However, ship owners were not prepared to run the gauntlet by committing their vessels to a daily game of Russian roulette in seas known to be infested by hostile submarines.

The government resolved the dilemma when it intervened and set up the Liverpool and London War Risk Association to provide emergency cover for the duration of the war. In essence, the government stepped in to provide insurance. Under the terms of War Risks, the Admiralty could dictate the course and speed of a ship, it could order it to run to the nearest harbour, or prevent it from leaving a harbour to meet its schedules. It could compel such a ship to turn around in mid-ocean and return to the port whence it had departed, to pick up last-minute errands or take on board regiments of troops or additional cargo. In many cases, the Admiralty's instructions were intended to protect ships when danger threatened, or to suggest counter measures that might deflect them away from the enemy. In issuing these orders, the Admiralty were not obliged to consult the ship owners who, on some occasions, resented not having a say in their own affairs; nor was any concern felt for disruption caused to often indignant passengers.

The consequences for ship owners ignoring these instructions were serious to say the least. A disobedient ship would automatically forfeit its right to insurance cover and ownership of the vessel would be forfeited by the government. Equally stringent regulations were in force in terms of the limited use imposed on merchant shipping wireless traffic. Admiralty control was so stringent that Cunard could not reach its own shipping directly by wireless for any purpose;

intended messages had first to be approved and then relayed via the Admiralty. Government wireless broadcasts to merchant ships fell broadly into two categories: transmissions to 'all ships' were pre-fixed CQ and would be sent in plain language or in cipher. The messages usually contained information relating to navigation, tidal conditions at certain ports, or instructions giving the course whereby they could evade the enemy. Regulations dictated that recipients of CQ messages could not acknowledge that they had received them. This was a perfectly logical precaution, as ships often betrayed their position to the enemy by use of their wireless. The other category of messages emanating from the Admiralty would be directed to a specific ship and usually called for acknowledgement. At the Mersey hearing, the London Commission and the New York Limits hearings, various wireless messages were examined in relation to the *Lusitania*. Without exception, these messages were in the CQ category and therefore addressed to all ships, not specifically to the *Lusitania,* as implied at the trial. However, the *Lusitania* also received five specific wireless messages addressed to the ship directly from the Admiralty between 6 and 7 May when she met her doom. The contents of these messages were never revealed, nor the telegrams located; however, some clues to their existence have survived in the archives. On 2 June 1915, the General Post Office in London responded to a request by the Admiralty for copies of messages sent specifically to the *Lusitania*. The Post Office letter states as follows:

GENERAL POST OFFICE
LONDON.

2nd June 1915

Sir,

I am directed by the Postmaster General to acknowledge the receipt of your letter of the 26th ultimo (NL) asking to be supplied, for the purposes of the enquiry which is about to be held into the circumstances of the loss of the steamship Lusitania, with copies of wireless messages sent to and received from that ship on Thursday sixth May and Friday seventh May by British coastal stations.

I am accordingly to send you herewith, for the information of the Lords Commissioners of the Admiralty, copies of five official radio-telegrams which have been traced as having been sent to, and their receipt acknowledged by, the ship at the times and on the dates shown thereon, and of one radio-telegram received at the Valentia coast station from the ship. The only other radio-telegram which can be traced as having been sent to or received from the ship on the dates in question is a private message addressed to a passenger which was apparently delivered on the sixth ultimo. As this has no bearing on the matter under enquiry, a copy is not forwarded …

The letter goes on to list other irrelevant enclosures such as extracts from logs of British coast stations from 17 April to 7 May 1915. The private message referred to was intended for Mr Vanderbilt and therefore irrelevant as the Post Office official had indicated in his letter to the Admiralty Secretary. Captain Turner referred briefly to the missing telegrams at the Kinsale Inquest the day after the *Lusitania* was torpedoed. Coroner Horgan, who headed the inquest, asked Turner if he had received any specific instructions from the Admiralty in relation to the navigation of his ship. Turner admitted that he had received such instructions but was not permitted to reveal their substance and referred the matter to the Admiralty. In 1917, a commission was set up in London to gather evidence for the New York Trial. A similar question of specific instructions from the Admiralty to the *Lusitania* was put to Turner who once more repeated that he could not answer the question because he would be in breach of instructions received.

In John Light's odyssey through the archives, he made a very intensive search for the five elusive Admiralty telegrams. Sometimes his hopes would be raised as he picked up the scent of a relevant MOD (Ministry of Defence) file, only to have them dashed again by the location of empty folders. John sensed the hand of the Admiralty at work as he pursued a trail to nowhere. One place from which the Admiralty failed to purge any clues about the messages' existence was, ironically, at the Admiralty itself. Under the MOD category of Home Water Telegrams, John Light located bound volumes of signals. Each volume typically contained signals transmitted over a four to five day period and averaging a total of 1,200–1,400 documents. These bulging volumes were drawn from the original War Registry Collection of all Admiralty Telegrams. In these volumes, John Light believed he would find the elusive signals and set about a search for messages from Queenstown, the Old Head signal station and Valentia, sent on the last critical two days of the *Lusitania*'s life. Frustration once more attended his search as he encountered gaps in the signal sequence; this was established by breaks in the various series and by insertion of blank numbered sheets in the telegraph volumes in place of missing messages. The inserts also fixed the approximate time of the missing signals as well as maintaining the chronological sequence of numbers in the file. The MOD admitted to John Light that the whereabouts of the missing signals could be traced back to 1972, but there the trail petered out. Patrick Beesly, author of *Room 40,* made an exhaustive and fruitless search for these signals as late as July 1982. In attempting to speculate as to the contents of the missing signals, it is worth considering hearsay evidence.

In John Light's crusade to unearth new clues, he visited the late Captain Turner's housekeeper and lifelong companion, Mabel Every, on a number of occasions, the last of which was in July 1973. John found Miss Every to be alert and sharp of memory, despite her years. Mabel Every was adamant that Turner had requested permission from the Admiralty to take the northern route around Ireland to Liverpool on the *Lusitania*'s final voyage. Presumably this request was submitted as he made landfall with the Irish coast. Miss Every did not know why Turner made this request, but stated that it was subsequently refused by the Admiralty. Had he chosen to ignore the Admiralty's refusal, the *Lusitania* might have been forfeited by the government under the terms of the War Risk Association conditions. Curiously Captain Turner's interrogator at the 1918 New York trial had raised the following question:

Q – If you had thought in the interests of the safety of the vessel and of your passengers to have taken the route by the North of Ireland, there was nothing to prevent you doing it?

A – As I said before, I cannot answer that question.

If we are to believe that Turner requested the northern route, then it seems most likely that his request was made on 6 May. We can therefore assume that the Admiralty made their refusal at a time when they had full knowledge of the threat posed by the U-20. They would certainly have known about the loss of the *Earl of Lathom* off Kinsale on 5 May, as well as the close encounter on the same evening between the steamer *Cayo Romano* and Schwieger's submarine. They may have known about the loss of at least one or both of the steamers sunk by Schwieger off the coast of Waterford on 6 May. They also had ten days' advance knowledge of Schwieger's intended patrol from Room 40 intercepts. If they had this knowledge, it seems extraordinary that they should refuse Turner's request and lead the unsuspecting *Lusitania* into a trap. A conspiracy theorist would see this action as a deliberate attempt to lure an innocent passenger liner to its doom. Was the Admiralty attempting to create circumstances that would embroil the great liner with Commander Schwieger of the U-20? Before we condemn the Admiralty out of hand, we must ask ourselves whether they had any good reason for refusing Turner's request to take the northern route. A study of this route relating to the first months of the war indicates that the Admiralty had ample reason for caution before recommending its use to vulnerable shipping.

On 26 October 1914, the Canadian-bound freighter, *Manchester Commerce,* was en route to Quebec, having departed from Manchester. She had cleared the North Irish channel around noon. Two hours later, she was steaming thirty miles off Donegal's Tory Island when she struck a German mine and sank with a loss of fourteen people, including the captain. The nearby coastguard station did not possess telegraphic equipment and there was a considerable lapse in time before news of the event was communicated to the Admiralty. The following morning found the British Navy's 23,000 ton Dreadnought class battleship, *Audacious,* steaming in the same area blissfully unaware of the misfortunes of the Canadian-bound freighter. This category of warship, in its heyday, was the most deadly and feared fighting machine afloat. Its armament consisted of ten 13.5-inch guns, sixteen 4-inch guns and four 3-pounders. These were awesome battleships, with guns bristling, they were the centre of attention and the envy of the world's greatest navies and they presaged a new era of war at sea. As the *Audacious* prepared to engage in squadron target practice, she struck a single mine which ripped her open below the waterline. The stricken battleship, hit on the aft port side, was nevertheless able to steam under her own power as she made for Lough Swilly. Her stern was sinking all the time as heavy seas broke over her. She later became unmanageable and her plight was observed by the passing 46,350-ton *Olympic,* who took the battleship in tow until the line parted in heavy seas; another attempt at towing was made by the collier, *Thornhill,* which also ended in failure. After a twelve-hour ordeal in buffeting seas, the stern of the *Audacious* was awash when the order was given to abandon ship. Every member of her 900 man crew made it ashore as the battleship turned upside-down, exploded and sank off the Donegal coast. It was later learned with some surprise that the German passenger liner, *Berlin,* had laid the minefield. This liner was owned by Norddeutscher Lloyd and had been requisitioned by the German government and converted to an armed merchant cruiser and minelayer in August 1914.

Both Royal Navy and Admiralty alike were stunned at what became the first Dreadnought casualty of the Great War. Only a month earlier, three British cruisers, *Aboukir, Hogue* and *Cressy* had been sent to the bottom of the North Sea by Otto Weddigen in the U-9 with a loss of 1,459 young British servicemen's lives. The Admiralty became infected with a great fear of submarines caused by the worsening situation, and were prone to developing the jitters with every fresh sighting of a periscope or mine. England charged Germany with indiscriminately scattering mines in the open sea on the main trade route from America to Liverpool via the north of Ireland, and retaliated by declaring the entire North Sea a military area. In effect, Britain had locked up the North Sea from 5 November 1914 and required all future shipping to use the Dover Straits, where they would be subject to having their cargoes searched and confiscated if it was deemed to be contraband for the enemy.

This was Britain's first attempt to cast a ring of steel around Germany, as they defended the new boundary by the use of patrolling warships of the Grand Fleet and the laying of minefields that would eventually stretch in a thirty-five-mile swathe from Scotland to the coast of Norway. The defence line was aptly named the Barrier of Death. Britain justified this exceptional measure as being the only way to protect peaceful commerce from the enemy's wanton and reckless endangerment. This was the start of a long and debilitating hunger blockade of Germany's citizens. On 19 December 1914, another merchant ship struck a mine and sank off Tory Island. Two days later, the Admiralty ordered all Atlantic merchant shipping to and from Irish seaports and Liverpool to proceed round the south of Ireland until further notice. This 'out-of-bounds' stretch of water was eventually swept and cleared of its mines and declared free once more for use by merchant ships on 26 April 1915, just four days before the *Lusitania* left New York for the last time. We do not know if Turner was granted clearance to take the optional northern route. Given the sluggish nature of Admiralty bureaucracy and its obsession with secrecy, it is possible that clearance instructions were still filtering through the system at Whitehall and had not reached Turner. As explained earlier, the various cells of information within the Admiralty worked in isolation of each other, and it is true to say that in certain instances, interdepartmental communication was non-existent. If, at some future date, a missing Admiralty telegram dissuading Turner from taking the northern route should come to light and confirm this hypothesis, little more will be confirmed than the veracity of Mabel Every's hearsay evidence to John Light. However, had the Admiralty admitted that such a refusal was made to Captain Turner it would have led many sceptics to draw very sinister conclusions about their reasons for doing so.

Yet another mystery attended the final voyage of the *Lusitania*. Some maintained that Captain Turner received last-minute instructions from the Admiralty to divert the *Lusitania* into Queenstown or, as conspiracy advocates would have it, into the arms of its nemesis, the German U-boat. Schwieger, the U-boat commander, attributed his good fortune in sinking the *Lusitania* to a course change made by Captain Turner which enabled him to converge on its track. In 1972, quartermaster Johnson, a survivor of the *Lusitania,* gave a television interview screened by the BBC and titled *Who sank the Lusitania*? On camera, Johnson unequivocally stated no less than three times that the *Lusitania* was heading for Queenstown when struck by Schwieger's death-dealing torpedo. This very salient piece of information was edited out of the final BBC production. Presumably it is still canned in the BBC archives; a full copy of the interview transcript is in the John Light archive. Johnson further stated that mails and baggage were being hauled out on deck in anticipation of the liner's arrival at Queenstown. Officers on the bridge had also dressed for port as a large body of Cunard crew members busied themselves below decks. At this stage, the *Lusitania*'s destination, Liverpool, was still 250 miles distant and over twelve hours away, given the liner's twenty-knot speed. The baggage handlers in the foreship had just slung the first cargo net of baggage and the winch man had taken a single turn of rope on the capstan head to commence lifting when the torpedo exploded and all the men below decks were tragically drowned. Two other survivors of the *Lusitania,* junior third officer Bestic and Leslie Morton, gave television interviews in a 1962 BBC production titled *Fifty Fathoms Deep,* and also an NBC production titled *Riddle of the Lusitania.* Their televised statements back up Johnson's claim that they were going down for mails and baggage at the time of the incident and would probably not have been doing so if the ship had intended a Liverpool stop only. Could another missing signal have contained an order to Turner to divert to Queenstown? We know of no logical reason for this instruction and can only examine previous diversions to find clues. Prior to the *Lusitania* incident, merchant ships were regularly diverted to Queenstown when danger threatened and were often ordered to remain in port for days until a destroyer escort could be made available to them. Did the Admiralty finally awake from their slumber and show concern for the safety of the *Lusitania* in view of the alarming losses of the previous two days in the same waters? Did it wish to divert the *Lusitania* into Queenstown until the danger had passed, or until it could provide an escort of destroyers to shepherd the liner to safety? If so, it was regrettable that their good intentions backfired and they inadvertently diverted the liner into the jaws of death in the form of Schwieger's torpedo. But why would the Admiralty wish to cover up this instruction at three different hearings? It should be remembered that, at the Mersey Tribunal, the main thrust of the Admiralty's condemnation of Turner was his disobedience of alleged orders in steering his ship too close to land. How could Turner have done otherwise? If he was instructed to make port, he would have no option but to close land as he made his approach. If such a revelation was made known to the Mersey Tribunal in June 1915, the main thrust of the Admiralty's case against Turner would have lost all validity. The fact that these telegrams have never been revealed tends to fuel suspicion that there was something to hide.

On 10 May, three days after the disaster, Churchill was obliged to make a statement in the House of Commons in relation to the sinking of the *Lusitania*. In anticipation of his speech, his assailants had armed themselves with a volley of questions. Lord Charles Beresford and others led the attack as members craned their necks to listen. What was the speed of the *Lusitania*? Was the Old Head patrolled? Had the Admiralty received the German warnings issued on the day of the voyage? Was it known that submarines were active in the region? Finally, was it not practice to meet and convoy steamers conveying horses, and if so, why not the *Lusitania*? Winston Churchill referred these matters to the Mersey hearing. Andrew Bonar Law, the leader of the opposition in the House, now intervened in the questioning and drew from Mr Churchill the disclosure that messages had been sent by the Admiralty to the *Lusitania* and had been acknowledged by the vessel, and that the last of these messages was timed a few minutes before the catastrophe. At this point, Churchill retreated with the comments, *'I will say nothing further pending the inquiry in case any discussion might be interpreted as implying blame on the captain.'* This last-minute message referred to by Churchill may well have been the hypothetical order to divert to Queenstown as claimed by Johnson; it is tantalising to guess the contents of the remaining three telegrams and the 'what if' scenarios become endless if we attempt to do so.

Could the *Lusitania* disaster be attributed to a lapse in Whitehall by the operations division (OD) of Admiralty Intelligence? Surely it is unthinkable that the Admiralty's silence reflected their gross inefficiency and condescending attitudes towards their brilliant team of civilian decoders at Room 40. Was over-centralisation and excessive secrecy in Whitehall the reason? Surely a system that depended entirely on the judgement and decisions of one man, Admiral Oliver, was flawed from the outset. The gulf of snobbery that existed between the operations division of the Admiralty and the codebreakers caused vital intelligence to be dissipated before reaching the Grand Fleet. If the loss of the *Lusitania* was attributable to an intelligence blunder in Whitehall, it was a relatively minor blunder when compared with that institution's performance throughout the Battle of Jutland in May twelve months later and, coincidentally, the anniversary month of the loss of the *Lusitania*.

During the first twenty-one months of the war, the main bulk of the German Navy stubbornly lurked at its anchorage in the Jade river at Wilhelmshaven, guarded by an immense minefield. Like their British counterparts, Germany looked upon its navy with great pride and did not wish to risk losing their valuable ships against the vastly superior forces of the Royal Navy. In May 1916, the German Navy, commanded by Admiral Scheer, at last began to bare its teeth and unknowingly betrayed its intentions, by excessive use of wireless, to break out and do battle. Room 40, who intercepted their wireless messages, accurately predicted, days in advance, that the long-awaited sea battle was about to happen. As early as 16 May, Room 40 detected sailings of German submarines which inexplicably failed to show up days later at the customary trades routes. Something strange was happening and Room 40 sensed that a major operation was imminent. On 28 and 29 May, Room 40 learned that the German Navy was ordered into a state of high alert. Observers at sea noted that German minesweepers were sweeping coastal waterways and barrier-breakers were also actively clearing sea lanes. Further signals indicated that the German Navy would put to sea in the early hours of 31 May and possibly at 3.40 a.m.

In the light of these new developments, the most powerful fleet in the world in 1916, the Royal Navy, led by its Commander-in-Chief, Admiral Sir John Jellicoe, and assisted by Commander David Beatty, put to sea from various Scottish ports in an assortment of ships ranging from Dreadnoughts, battlecruisers, armoured cruisers, destroyers, minelayers, light cruisers and a solitary seaplane carrier. In total, 149 British warships of the Grand Fleet departed for war with a complement of 60,000 men. In the great battle to come the following day, one in every ten men would die. Armed with valuable intelligence, the Grand Fleet would not be caught off guard and was already at sea and prepared for action several hours before their adversaries left port. The German Navy, led by Scheer, numbered 99 warships, 18 submarines, and 45,000 men by comparison. Room 40 intercepted a message on 31 May telling them that the German fleet was now on the high seas and steaming for battle. As was usual practice in Whitehall, this message was passed on to the operations division of the Admiralty who would interpret its contents and then relay their findings to the Grand Fleet in the North Sea. The message contained a call-sign transfer which OD recklessly misinterpreted. Unbelievably, the message that was relayed to Jellicoe just before noon on 31 May stated that the German fleet was still in port, at anchorage when, in fact, it was already several hours at sea. On receipt of this message, Jellicoe found himself with spare time on his hands which he used by making routine searches of merchant ships and engaging in other trivial duties; in so doing, he achieved little more than wasting precious fuel and daylight.

As he peered through the mists of the North Sea, he was stunned by disbelief when he discovered the entire German Navy bearing down on him; his confidence in Admiralty Intelligence was severely shaken as a result. The huge armada of fighting ships from both navies that had steamed to battle off the coast of Denmark totalled 248 ships and covered an enormous expanse of sea. As the fleets closed range on each other on 31 May, bright gun-muzzle flashes from seemingly invisible ships beyond the horizon heralded the start of a very confusing and ferocious battle that was fought in three parts. First was a running fight between the battlecruisers; this was followed by encounters between Dreadnoughts and their colossal guns; and ended in a night battle when confusion was complete. Room 40 participated throughout and found that the level of wireless transmissions intensified from 9.25 p.m. on 31 May onwards into the confused night. The codebreakers learned from intercepts that the eighteen-strong fleet of submarines was instructed to take up new positions; instructions were also issued to German destroyers to bring them into more favourable attack positions against the Grand Fleet, as well as information about the disposition of ships. None of these vital and possibly lifesaving signals was passed to Jellicoe. Throughout the battle, a vast expanse of the North Sea was aflame from the burning ships as volleys of giant shells screamed through the air seeking their targets. Some fell short and crashed into the sea, sending large plumes of water and vapour skywards; others exploded on impact with devastating consequences. Bursting shells shredded human life on an unprecedented scale and washed the decks red with their blood. Gun-turrets were torn from their mountings and decks twisted into unrecognisable heaps of buckled steel and scrap metal. Both British and German warships dashed hither and thither in this rain of death. As ships were blasted to pieces, many caught fire and subsequently exploded as flame reached their magazines. A deafening thunder of guns and bursting shells filled the air as burning and sinking ships sent dense clouds of smoke curling hundreds of feet skywards. The crackling sound of burning decks was accompanied by the acrid smell of cordite, with visibility obscured by the smoke from the ships adding further to the confusion. So violent was the explosion of one ship's magazine that it sliced the vessel in two and the separate halves stood on end like giant headstones for over half-an-hour before being engulfed by the sea. Many ships had their engines and rudders disabled by the relentless salvoes from the Dreadnoughts and drifted aimlessly out of control in the mêlée of battle.

By late evening, Admiral Scheer, realising that he was heavily outnumbered and that his ships had taken very severe punishment, decided to disengage and make for Wilhelmshaven. To continue the battle the following day, 1 June, against the might of Britain's superior navy would be nothing short of suicide. His chances of safe return were very slim indeed as by now Jellicoe had positioned the Grand Fleet between Scheer's navy and his route home to Germany. As Scheer took stock of his desperate situation and his battered fleet, he realised that his only chance was a night-time death-or-glory breakthrough of the British lines of destroyers. Under cover of darkness, Scheer made his dash for home as he fought a series of bloody battles with British destroyers and cruisers in the confused blackness of night. In these sorties, his ships took further severe pounding from British guns. Scheer had considered four possible routes as he contemplated his return. However, he chose the shortest route which was the same as the one he had taken on the way out, namely the Horns Reef route. Room 40 learned of his intention from an intercept. This time Admiralty OD relayed the message correctly to Jellicoe who discarded it with some justification in view of the gross misinformation he had received earlier, advising that the German fleet was in port.

Scheer's successful dash through enemy lines heralded the end of one of the greatest sea battles fought in history. In a matter of a few hours, Britain had suffered the loss of three battle cruisers, three armoured cruisers and eight destroyers. In total, fourteen warships of the Grand Fleet had gone to the bottom of the ocean, claiming the lives of 6,000 British servicemen. This was not the result the Admiralty had anticipated and prompted Churchill to remark that Jellicoe was the only man capable of losing the war in a single afternoon. Germany, by comparison, lost eleven ships and 2,500 servicemen. The battle was inconclusive, with both sides claiming victory.

At 9.40 p.m., Room 40 intercepted another German wireless message from Admiral Scheer, ordering Zeppelin reconnaissance of the Horns Reef route in support of his return voyage. This was copper-fastened proof of Scheer's intentions. Inexplicably, this vital piece of intelligence was not passed on to Jellicoe or the Grand Fleet. Had Jellicoe received this information, it would have clinched his views about the earlier decode of Scheer's route home. Jellicoe was already in a very favourable position to start the attack again on 1 June. Had he received the accurate intelligence, which was in the hands of the Admiralty, he might well have annihilated a great portion of the badly-mauled German fleet with its severely damaged battle cruisers as they limped for home. Jellicoe inadvertently assisted Scheer to make his escape by incorrectly estimating that his adversary would return via the Ems channel. A large body of Jellicoe's ships steered south for the Ems and thus further away from Scheer. British Intelligence had learned from an intercept that the Germans believed the Ems channel to be mined and therefore out-of-bounds to German shipping. Like so many other vital signals, the Ems intercept never left the Admiralty. Had this vital signal been made known to Jellicoe, it would have precluded his making the wrong decision. As dawn broke on 1 June, Scheer had broken through the British warships and was safely back in Wilhelmshaven. On that morning, a deathly stillness had descended on the North Sea and as Jellicoe scanned the horizon, he found an ocean empty of German battleships but littered with corpses and wreckage from the previous day's Armageddon.

A few days later, on 4 June, Jutland claimed another victim in a curious twist of fate. A minefield laid for the battle was responsible for the loss of the HMS *Hampshire* en route to Russia on a mission of diplomacy. Lord Kitchener, the Secretary of State for War, was on board at the time and consequently lost his life when an exploding mine sent the ship to the bottom.

In later analysis of the Horns Reef blunder, some experts believe that it may have been attributed to the jaded and overworked Admiral Oliver taking to his bed for some much-needed sleep at this critical time.

He may have appointed an inexperienced stand-in to take his place; if he did, if was obviously someone who could not appreciate the importance of what was asked of him and was not up to the job. If one considers that the Admiralty worked with the speed of a lame tortoise when their operations division received the Horns Reef decode at 10.10 p.m., and even allowing for their inexcusably long delays in passing on information, the contents of that signal would still have proved invaluable to Jellicoe if transmitted as late as 1.15 a.m. on the following day, 1 June. This would have enabled Jellicoe sufficient time to renew the attack on Germany under very favourable conditions and with every prospect of destroying a great portion of their wounded fleet. A priceless opportunity had been thrown away in a reckless and perfidious manner.

Throughout the Jutland incident, the Admiralty's performance was irresponsible to say the least. Later studies of the Intelligence debacle revealed that, as usual, the lower echelons of Room 40, the civilian codebreakers, had performed in an exemplary manner. Between 9.55 p.m. on 31 May and 3.00 p.m. on 1 June, no fewer than sixteen Room 40 decodes from Scheer's fleet had been passed to the Admiralty's operations division. Each of these decodes would have added greatly to Jellicoe's knowledge of the unfolding situation. Incredibly, only three of the sixteen decodes were passed to Jellicoe, including the misleading message advising that the German Navy was still in port. Britain, which had superiority from the start in terms of ships and men and was backed with priceless intelligence, should have had a sweeping victory. If the system that Churchill had devised was responsible for allowing the *Lusitania* to steam to its doom, it is extraordinary that Admiral Oliver and his cohorts had learnt nothing from the lesson and continued to dither until they had achieved the biggest intelligence blunder of the First World War, in the Battle of Jutland.

In exploring this slice of history, the scrutiny of its central figures has been most revealing. In attempting to draw conclusions about these characters, it is easy to be of two minds about the actions of Walter Schwieger; was he an evil villain and mass murderer of innocent civilians, or just another submariner who realised that the age of chivalry had ended? Like many of his colleagues, he may have realised that one tended to live longer by shooting first and asking questions later. Did Schwieger harbour doubts about the *Lusitania* concealing guns that might open fire at any moment, with lethal consequences for him and his crew? If he had dallied, and shown concern first for human life by challenging the *Lusitania* and offering the passengers the opportunity to abandon ship before launching his torpedo, he may well have precipitated his own demise at the hands of a hostile liner, whose captain had secret orders to ram enemy submarines. If the *Lusitania*'s cargo had not included a highly explosive 46-ton shipment of aluminium fine powder, the second explosion would not have occurred, and the liner might well have made it to port in a crippled condition. Loss of life would have been minimal, and the incident would have been recorded as a minor event in the annals of war.

In making his decision to torpedo the *Lusitania,* Schwieger would have known about the fate of the German liner *Cap Trafalgar,* which was sunk by gunfire from the British armed liner *Carmania* off Trinidade in 1914. This Cunard liner underwent a rapid metamorphosis on the eve of war, when it was converted to a twelve-gun warship. It is likely that Schwieger would have known about the emplacement of guns around the decks of the *Aquitania* and other passenger liners. He may have known that the *Lusitania* was a gunrunner, as a result of information gleaned from German spies in New York; and as such, she would have been a legitimate target of war. Schwieger had displayed chivalry while sinking the schooner, the *Earl of Lathom,* and the steamer *Candidate,* by allowing the crew and its passengers to abandon ship. Did he opt for this gallant method of sinking those ships because he felt it was safe to do so in those cases, but that other factors governed the *Lusitania*? His motives will never be understood, as he carried them to his grave in 1917, when an exploding British mine sank his submarine, the U-88, with all hands.

Events in Captain Turner's life indicate that he was a brave and conscientious man. His various awards and merits; his plunging into the freezing Mersey in mid-winter to rescue a drowning boy; his mid-Atlantic rescue of the crew of a burning ship, *West Point*. These are hardly the actions of a captain who was later accused of negligence, disobedience, and the reckless handling of the *Lusitania* in a war zone. On the contrary, if we consider the hearsay evidence of Mabel Every to John Light, we can assume he was an obedient officer who accepted the Admiralty's judgement when they refused his request to take the northern route as he neared Fastnet.

In considering the further hearsay evidence of Officer Johnson to John Light, we may assume that Turner obeyed an Admiralty instruction to divert to Queenstown. It would seem that Turner was an honest man, who was traduced by the Admiralty in order to conceal their own shortcomings in safeguarding the *Lusitania*.

Winston Churchill deserves recognition for his instantaneous appreciation of the value of the *Magdeburg* codes, which led to his subsequent wisdom in setting up the codebreaking division known as Room 40, in Whitehall. It is regrettable that his obsession with excessive secrecy had the effect of fettering the brilliant team of cryptographers who worked within that department and who caused much valuable information to be needlessly dissipated through a flawed system.

There is no evidence that Churchill conspired to sink the *Lusitania* in a bid to entice neutral America to enter the war on the Allied side. However, with hindsight, he would have seen the benefits of the tragedy in heightening anti-German sentiment world-wide, and influencing American public opinion in favour of the Allied cause. The massacre of 1,198 lives was a minute statistic when compared with daily losses in the trenches of Europe. In those final days leading up to the sinking of the *Lusitania,* Churchill would have been immersed in the failing Gallipoli campaign which he had largely masterminded. He was also preoccupied with trying to devise some means to entice the Imperial German Navy out to face the British Grand Fleet and, he hoped, certain annihilation in a great sea battle. He felt sure that such a victory would break the stalemate in the trenches, and stem the haemorrhaging of Winston Churchill's rapidly expiring career as First Lord of the Admiralty.

It is to be hoped that the fog of confusion sur-rounding many of the issues relating to the sinking of the *Lusitania* – the second mystery explosion, the exact nature of the munitions cargo on board the ship, the disguising of the ship's manifest, how evidence was concocted within the Admiralty to scapegoat Captain Turner, the rigging of the sham tribunals, the inexplicable failure of Room 40 to act throughout the affair, and their reluctance to warn the oncoming

Lusitania of the grave danger known to lay in its path – has been lifted. The jigsaw is almost complete. However, one or two tantalising pieces are still missing, and one hopes that the cloak of secrecy that has lain over the *Lusitania* for the last almost hundred years will some day be lifted by the finding of the five vital signals sent specifically to the *Lusitania* from the Admiralty, during the last two days of its final voyage. New revelations may well, finally, exonerate Captain Turner. Truth will out, and one hopes that some future investigator, blessed with John Light's dogged determination and Sherlock-Holmes-like intuition, will at last bring the *Lusitania* story to a dignified conclusion.

Archival Sources

British Admiralty Documents (In Public Record Office, Kew)

Ship's logs (men-o-war)
ADM – 53/33908, *Aquitania* (AMC) (7 August–
3 September 1914)
ADM – 53/46309, *Laverock* (TBD)
ADM – 53/47326, *Louis* (TBD)

Admiralty Case Histories
ADM – 116/1416, *Lusitania Case History*

Home Waters Telegrams
ADM – 137/98 (1–5 March 1915)
ADM – 137/99 (6–9 March 1915)
ADM – 137/108 (25–30 April 1915)
ADM – 137/112 (1–4 May 1915)
ADM – 137/113 (5–10 May 1915)

War History Volumes
ADM – 137/385, *Baralong, War History*
ADM – 137/969, *Policy, Armed Merchant Cruisers*
ADM – 137/423, *Grand Fleet Narrative*

ADM – 137/818, (*Armed Merchant Cruisers*)
ADM – 137/1011, (*Armed Boarding Vessels*)
ADM – 137/1050, *Q–ship Operations*
ADM – 137/1057, *Operations Irish Sea, 1915, 1st Half*
ADM – 137/1058, *Lusitania War History*
ADM – 137/1060, *U–boats, South West Approaches*
ADM – 137/1681, *Armed Merchants Cruiser, Policy*

IDHS Volumes (in ADM – 137 class)
ADM – 137/3865, *German Submarine Technical Manual*
(NID translation)
ADM – 137/3923, *U-20's Log* (photocopy obtained 1920)
ADM – 137/3956, *Current Log* (12 April–5 May 1915)
ADM – 137/3958, *North Sea Diary* (1 January–30 April
1915)
ADM – 137/3959, *North Sea Diary* (1 May–31 July 1915)
ADM – 137/4101, *U–boat Messages* (Reports of U-boat
sightings and actions received in War room:
16 April–31 May 1915)
ADM – 137/4152, *History Sheets* (IDHS Current
movement logs of U14–U23)
ADM – 186/678, *Merchant Vessel Code, 1st Edition*

Board of Trade Documents
MT – 23, 400/T24946/1915
MT – 9–1326

Foreign Office
F.O. – 115/1996
F.O. – 371/2587

Hall Papers, Churchill College, Cambridge, England

Archival Sources

American Sources

National Archives, Washington D.C.

State Department

Microcopy 580, Rolls 197–198

Justice Department

Record Group 8, 9140-646, File MI–4–17–Aug./18,
(Synopsis Franz von Rintelen)

Office of U.S. Naval Intelligence (ONI)
(Microfilm Records of Captured German Naval Documents)

Roll T – 1022–3, U-boat Logs:
   U-14 (30 July–4 November 1914), pp.61518; *U-20*
      (2 August–31 December 1914), pp.61532; *U-20*
      (1 January–17 March 1915) pp.61533.
   Roll T – 1022–4, U-boat Logs; *U-20,* (18 March–31
      August 1915), pp.61535
   Roll T – 1022–26, U-boat Logs: *U-35,*
      (16 April–15 November 1915), pp.61577.
   Roll T-1022-32, U-boat Logs: *U-27,* (31 July 1914–
      4 August 1915) pp.61556

National Archives and Records Administration, N.Y.

   ADM – 61–169 (Cunard's Limits of Liability Hearings,
      1918)

Library of Congress, Washington, D.C.

   Paper of *Chandler P. Anderson, Reel 1, July 22, 1915*

Yale University Library, New Haven, CT.

   Papers of *Colonel Edward M. House*

Bibliography

The Adventure of Sail, Ferndale Editions, London 1979

The Aquitania, L.&R.A. Streater, The Maritime Publishing Co. 1997

Battles by Sea, E. Keble Chatterton, Sidgwick and Jackson Ltd. 1925

Beating the U-Boats, E. Keble Chatterton, Hurst & Blackett Ltd. 1943

Bridge to Engine Room, Captain A.C. Douglas, Sea Breezes 1997

Chronicle of the 20th. Century, Dorling Kindersley Books 1995

Churchill and Secret Service, David Stafford, P. John Murray, London 1997

Dictionary of Disasters at Sea, Vols 1–2, Charles Hocking, F.L.A. 1967

Dreadnought, Richard Hough, Michael Joseph Ltd. 1964

Exploring the Lusitania, Robert Ballard, Madison Press 1995

Famous Liners of the Past, Laurence Dunn, Patrick Stephens Ltd.

Famous Sea Battles, D. Howard, Little, Brown & Co. 1981

The First World War, Martin Gilbert, HarperCollins 1995

Germany and the Approach to War in 1914, V.R. Berghahn, Macmillan 1993

The Great War, Vols 2–12, H.W. Wilson, London Amalgamated Press 1915–1922

History of Ships, New English Library Vols. 1–4

History of the First World War, Liddell Hart, Papermac 1992

A History of the Twentieth Century, Vol 1, 1900–1933, Martin Gilbert, HarperCollins 1997

Bibliography

The Killing Time, the German U-Boats 1914–1918, Edwyn A. Gray, Seeley Service, London 1972

The Last Voyage of the Lusitania, Hoehling and Hoehling, circa 1956

The Liners, Rob McAuley, Boxtree 1997

The Liners, Terry Coleman, Penguin 1976

The Liverpool Pals, Graham Maddocks, Wharncliff Publishers 1993

Lusitania, Patrick Stephens 1986

The Lusitania *Case,* Tantum and Droste, Patrick Stephens Ltd. 1972

The Lusitania *Disaster,* Thomas A. Bailey and Paul B. Ryan, The Free Press 1975

Majesty at Sea, John H. Shaum Jr. & William H. Flayhart 3rd, Patrick Stephens 1981

Mediterranean Submarines, Michael Wilson & Paul Kemp, Crecy Publishing Ltd. 1997

A Merchant Fleet at War, Archibald Hurd, Cassell & Co. 1920

My Mystery Ships, Rear Admiral Gordon Cambell, Hodder & Stoughton 1929

A Naval History of World War 1, Paul G. Halpern, UCL Press 1994

Q Ships and their story, E. Keeble Chatterton, Sidgwick and Jackson Ltd. 1922

Roger Keyes, C. Aspinall Oglander, The Hogarth Press 1951

Room 40, British Naval Intelligence 1914–18, Patrick Beesly, Hamilton & Hamilton 1982

Royal Air Force and United States Naval Air service in Ireland 1913–1923

The Sea and the Easter Rising, Dr John De Courcy Ireland

Seven Days to Disaster, Des Hickey and Gus Smith, Collins, London 1981

The Shipbuilder, Vols 1–2, Mark D. Warren, Blue Riband Publishers 1995

The Sinking of the Lusitania

A Short History of the World, H.G. Wells, Penguin 1965

The Story of the Submarine, Antony Preston, Octopus Books 1975

Submarines and the War at Sea 1914–1918, Richard Compton-Hall, Macmillan 1991

Submarines, Anthony Preston, Bison Books Ltd. 1982

THS Journal, Ed Kamuda, Quarterly

The Tragedy of the Lusitania, Captain Frederick D. Ellis 1915

Triumph of the Edwardian Era, Eric Sauder and Ken Marschall 1990

Tumult in the Clouds, Nigel Steel & Peter Hart, Hodder & Stoughton 1997

U-Boat Intelligence, 1914–1918, Robert M. Grant, Putnam, London 1969

The U-Boat, Eberhard Rossler, Arms and Armour Press 1981

Warships, Bernard Ireland, Hamlyn 1978

Wartime Disasters at Sea, David Williams, Patrick Stephens Ltd.

The World Crisis, W. Churchill, Thornton Butterworth 1931

Papers:

John Light Papers

Lusitania Shock Wave, Dermot Lucey MA

Patrick Beesly Papers

Robson Papers, Trinity College, Dublin

The Inflammability of Aluminium Dust, Alan Leighton Edwards, Bureau of Mines

Transcript of interview, Ludovic Kennedy with Captain Stephen Roskill

Newspapers:

Southern Star

The Sunday Times

Index

Index

Index

Index